SEVEN DEADLY SINS

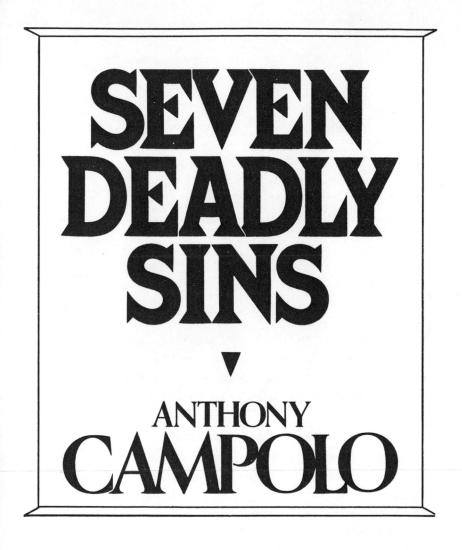

SEVEN DEADLY SINS

▼

ANTHONY CAMPOLO

VICTOR BOOKS™

A DIVISION OF SCRIPTURE PRESS PUBLICATIONS INC.
USA CANADA ENGLAND

Scripture quotations are from *The Holy Bible: Revised Standard Version,* © 1946, 1952, 1971, 1973; and from the *King James Version* (KJV).

Recommended Dewey Decimal Classification: 233.2
  Suggested Subject Heading: SIN

Library of Congress Catalog Card Number: 86-63137
ISBN: 0-89693-533-7

VICTOR BOOKS A division of SP Publications, Inc. Wheaton, Illinois 60187

CONTENTS

To Robert and Dorothy Davidson,
my brother-in-law and sister-in-law,
who model servanthood for the people
of Chesterfield Baptist Church

PREFACE

SLOTH. LUST. ANGER. PRIDE. ENVY. GLUTTONY. GREED.
The church leaders of the Middle Ages named them The
Seven Deadly Sins. They urged people to purge themselves of
these sins, for they knew that out of them came the evil in the
world. But they are not so much sins as they are evil disposi-
tions which motivate us to sin. They are attitudes, emotions,
and states of mind which condition our behavior in ways that
are destructive to ourselves and to those who are around us.

It is quite correct to say that we sin because we are sinners.
Even before we do anything that is contrary to the will of God
or act in ways that bring pain and sorrow into the lives of
others, we are possessors of sinful natures which make our sin
inevitable. Theologians in the evangelical tradition call this
inner spiritual condition *original sin.* They point out that we
are born sinners. Each of us comes into the world with a
predisposition to live in such a way as to inflict pain on those
who love us most, and to offend the God who cares for us
infinitely.

What the medieval church leaders knew, social scientists are
only now belatedly admitting: that we are all sinners by nature
and are helpless to be otherwise. No commitment to do good
will last. No New Year's resolution will long be upheld. No
determination to overcome evil will succeed. The *bad news* is
that unless something miraculous happens, we will continue
to do the evil that we have always done because there is

9

something basically wrong with what we are. The *good news* is that God is willing to perform a miracle—He wants to change our basic nature. He is willing to invade our personalities and make us into new creatures. As a matter of fact, it is this miracle that God wants to carry out in us which is our only hope.

Only through this miracle can we become persons who are inclined to do good and be a blessing to others. This miracle is what Christians call salvation. God wants each of us to experience it. The same Jesus who died on the cross as He was being punished for our sins was resurrected from the dead three days later. He is with us now, even as He promised He would be. If any of us chooses to invite Him to be a personal friend, this Jesus will enter into a personal transforming relationship with that person.

There is nothing that any of us have to do to earn our salvation because all that was necessary to atone for our sins was done for us 2,000 years ago on Calvary's cross. But there is more to salvation than simply accepting the propositional truth that Jesus died for our sins. To experience the salvation of God, each of us must individually invite the resurrected Jesus to effect an inner transformation of our personalities. This lifelong process wherein we are radically changed is called *sanctification*. It is through this process that salvation is worked out in our personal lives (Phil. 2:12-13). The process of being transformed into persons who possess the holiness of Jesus takes a lifetime, so that none of us is ever able to claim to have arrived spiritually. Even the Apostle Paul said, "Brethren, I do not consider that I have made it my own; but one thing I do, forgetting what lies behind and straining forward to what lies ahead, I press on toward the goal for the prize of the upward call of God in Christ Jesus" (Phil. 3:13-14).

We reach spiritual perfection only after death, when we are glorified into the likeness of Christ. "Beloved, we are God's children now; it does not yet appear what we shall be, but we know that when He appears we shall be like Him, for we shall see Him as He is" (1 John 3:2).

The gradual process of sanctification is what this book is all about. Because transformation into the likeness of Christ is of ultimate concern to the Christian, an understanding of the Seven Deadly Sins is of great significance. With the help of the Holy Spirit, we must leave these marks of our former life behind and become more and more like Jesus.

This book about sin could not have been written without the help of some saints. Mary Noel Keough, my secretary, did typing and Beverly Carlson did proofreading and editing. Carole Streeter put this book in its final form and came up with all the necessary sectional subtitles. Finally, there is my wife, Peggy, who makes everything I do possible. I do not want to *blame* this book on these good people, but I am grateful to them for their help.

Tony Campolo
St. Davids, Pennsylvania
1987

CHAPTER ONE

SLOTH

THE FIRST OF the Seven Deadly Sins is sloth which, in the modern vernacular, means laziness. It may surprise us that this sin is at the top of the list.* We tend to think of laziness as a weakness or a common human fault. Those of us raised according to the Protestant work ethic see laziness as an undesirable trait. Sloth is something we make jokes about. However, few of us would list it as a major sin.

We look on laziness as a cultural trait that enables us to jest wistfully about those people who appear to have a more "relaxed" attitude toward work than Type A personalities who are on their way to becoming workaholics. Listing sloth as the first of Seven Deadly Sins may seem a little extreme. Those with politically leftist leanings might even consider the designation of sloth on this list of crucial sins to be an attempt by capitalists to use religion as an instrument for condemning any who are not enthusiastic members of the work force. Nevertheless, this designation of the church fathers may have genuine validity.

M. Scott Peck, a social scientist who has written some of the most popular books in the field of psychotherapy, would concur with their assessment of sloth. Peck says that laziness is a major cause of evil, a primary cause of psychological illness, and the main reason that Americans are increasingly failing at human relations.

LAZINESS IN LOVING

First of all, Peck points out that laziness is what prevents us from being loving, and we all know that failure to be loving has horrendous consequences in our world. Love requires commitment and work, and those who are lazy are seldom willing to expend that kind of energy. For the lazy of the world, love is something that is just supposed to happen. As the song suggests, "Some enchanted evening, you will see a stranger. . . . and somehow you'll know. . . . " Most popular songs make love seem like an accident. Our culture promotes a view of love that makes this most important characteristic of being human and of being Christian seem to be a spontaneous emotion which can be neither controlled nor created.

When youngsters ask their parents how they will know when they are "in love," they receive the standard answer: "When you're in love, you'll know!" This failure to recognize that love is an art requiring discipline and hard work is largely responsible for the absence of love in so many of our interpersonal relationships. Nowhere is the lovelessness caused by laziness more evident than in the array of broken marriages in our society. Love becomes nonexistent and marriages collapse primarily because most people do not work hard enough to create love and build marital relationships.

I agree with Peck's analysis. In my limited experience as a counselor, I too have found laziness to be the major cause for the failure of marriages. Time and time again, I have observed that the parties involved in marital disputes have known exactly what was needed to restore the relationship, but were unwilling to put forth the effort. Time and time again, I have been told by marital partners on the verge of separation that they just did not want to do what was necessary to create something positive out of what had become the "empty shell" of a relationship. Some claimed that they had tried too many times already and decided to give up rather than try again. Others have copped out with fatalistic statements such as, "This marriage was just not meant to be." Still others have assumed that they were incompatible with their mates. In almost every case, those whose marriages failed simply were too lazy to do what was necessary to make their marital relationships work.

In one particular case, the husband had become preoccupied with sports. When he was in high school, he played on the basketball and football teams. In the early years of marriage, his wife tried to share his interest. She went to games with him and cheered for the hometown professional teams. She regularly read the sports pages of the newspapers in order to be informed enough to carry on conversations with her husband about how the players and teams were doing; but his interest in sports grew until it became a total preoccupation. Nothing else in life seemed to interest him. His sexual interest in his wife diminished. His involvement in church declined and there was room for nothing else in his life but sports.

One day his wife left him for another man. He came to me to see if there was something he could do to get her back. I told him that there *was* something he could do. He could change. I told him that he could cut back on the time and energy he spent on being a sports fanatic and make a commitment to his wife to give time and attention to things that would interest her. I told him that he would have to rearrange the priorities in his life and begin to give the Lord and his family the time and attention they deserved. He listened to me for a while and then said, "I thought of all that; but to tell the truth, I don't feel it's worth the effort. I want her back, but not that much."

The case may seem a little extreme, but I assure you it is not. All across this country, sports are moving from pastime to preoccupation. More and more people (usually men) are allowing the games of their favorite teams to become the most important events in their lives. Too lazy to get out of the stuffed chairs that seem riveted in front of their television sets, vicariously involved in the exploits of their favorite stars, they become passive observers of the play of others, and feel they have done something significant when their teams win.

It is time that church leaders recognize that spectator sports are nurturing a latent tendency to laziness in the lives of their members. It is time that we all become aware that precious time is being absorbed by a sports mania that threatens devotion to God and to family. How many hours that are desperately needed for building relationships between parents and children are being consumed in the TV football games? How many Monday nights are lost to the pro game of the week? How many New Year's Days are turned into a meaningless progression of bowl games?

When these lazy observers of other people's activities are told about this encroaching evil in their lives, they joke about it. They know that what they are doing is a wrongful waste of precious time. They recognize that their mates and children are being denied one of the most precious gifts that can be given. Nevertheless, they refuse to change. Sloth prevents them from escaping from their lazy preoccupations and from paying attention to that which has eternal significance. They know better, but they are too lazy to do anything about it. Sloth makes what is of ultimate importance seem not worth the effort. The case of this derelict husband can be duplicated by hundreds of thousands across the country.

LAZINESS, LOVE, AND WILL

I knew a woman who was going through a psychological hell. She was suffering from depression that seemed to be getting progressively worse. Her husband brought her to me believing that unless she received some help, she might hurt herself in some way or even commit suicide.

The first two sessions that I had with her revealed nothing that might be the cause of her neurotic condition. During the third visit, I took a shot in the dark and asked her, "Are you having a sexual affair?" She hesitated for a long time, then said, "Yes," and broke down in tears.

This woman had come from a Christian background and was still actively involved in the life of the church. She held to a conservative theological and ethical system of thought and was well aware of God's judgment on what she was doing. Furthermore, she was aware of the connection between her illicit affair and her depression. She did not need me to point out the nexus between what she was doing and how she was feeling. She understood all too well that there would be no deliverance from her depression until she repented of her sin and got right with God. I asked her why she did not do what she knew she had to do to find an escape from her dire straights. She answered, "You don't understand—I am in love. Losing him would be too painful for me to bear. What you are asking is too hard. I just can't do it."

Life is not easy. It is hard to do the will of God. Setting one's life right through repentance is not a happy experience. But if one is too lazy to do what one knows has to be done, there will result a deadness to the heart and soul that psychotherapy cannot cure. Sloth is the demonic tendency to remain where we are when we ought to be moving on to do those things which we know will provide deliverance from the pain of our existence.

When I counsel someone who is about to walk out on a marriage partner, I ask, "Do you *want* to be in love with your spouse? Do you *want* to be turned on by your mate?" Usually I am told that questions like these are ridiculous, that people cannot *make* themselves love those for whom they feel nothing. They claim that when love is dead, nothing can be done about it.

After listening to their protestations, I point out that when the Bible describes love, it almost always speaks of something that is willed. Husbands are *commanded* to love their wives. Wives are *commanded* to love their husbands. All people are *commanded* to love their neighbors. There is no doubt about the fact that Jesus spoke of love as something that people should *do;* and if love is something we should do, then lazy people, who are unwilling to put forth the effort to love, are justifiably condemned by our Lord.

I challenge those who come to me for marriage counseling this way: "If you do what I tell you to do for an entire month, I can promise you that by the end of the month, you will be in love with your mate. Are you willing to give it a try?" It is amazing to me how many clients who try to plead that they are not primarily responsible for the breakup of their marriage refuse to accept this challenge. They act as though they are victims of broken marriages when, in reality, they too are causing the demise of the relationship because they are too lazy to do what I ask them to do. They see divorce as an easier alternative than working hard at bringing a dead relationship to life again.

When couples accept my challenge, the results are invariably successful. I offer neither a sophisticated scientific discovery nor a magical formula. My prescription for creating love is so simple that those to whom I give it often scoff at what I tell. "Do ten things each day that you would do if you really were in love," I tell them. "First thing in the morning, make a list of ten specific things you could do that day to express your love if you were in love." I know that if people do loving things, it will not be long before they experience the feelings that are often identified as being in love. Love is not those feelings. Love is what one wills *to do* to make the other person happy and fulfilled. Doing those things generates the feelings which are associated with "being in love." In our society, we believe that what a person *feels* influences what he does. Often, we don't realize that what a person *does* influences what he feels.

I tell clients who are trying to recreate positive marital relationships to take the time to write love notes and to say sweet things to their partners. If they make the effort to express love, it will not be long before they feel love.

The story is told of a couple who came to a marriage counselor. At the end of the session, the wife said sadly, "I can't remember the last time my husband said, 'I love you.' "

"Is that true?" the counselor inquired.

With some anger in his voice, the husband said, "The day I married her I said, 'I love you,' and I told her that if I ever changed my mind, I'd let her know."

Within the story, his answer is meant to be funny, but its real-life implications are tragic. By not saying our love, we let it die. Love must be expressed in words and deeds in order to be revitalized and grow.

TOO LAZY TO NURTURE

Most of the problems related to rearing children in our modern world are caused by sloth. Children become undisciplined because parents are too lazy to do the hard work associated with nurturing them properly in the ways of responsible living. Many parents have given up on trying to get their children to straighten their rooms and make their beds because their children do not readily follow orders. Parents tell me that it is easier to take care of their children's rooms than to get them to do it themselves. They explain that after trying repeatedly with little success, they give up. I point out to such parents that they are lazy, and that by their own admission, they are unwilling to keep at their responsibility until things are done right. Everybody knows that the most important thing is not the straightening of rooms, but the disciplining of children to do what they are supposed to do, even when they don't feel like it. The parents who do not keep at the task of requiring their children to do what is expected of them, and who find it too much trouble to be checking constantly on them, are too lazy themselves to do for their children what God requires of them.

Knowing that they can get lazy parents to do the work that they should do, some children deliberately try to drive their parents to the point of such exasperation that they'll say, "Never mind, I'll do it myself." They test their parents to see how hard they are willing to try to get them to work. Usually, they find that their parents have so little perseverance that they choose the easiest course, which is to relieve their children of responsibility.

I can remember as a boy being told that it was my job to the dishes after dinner. My first response was to pretend that I did not know how to wash them and that I could not learn. My mother proceeded to show me how, and I pretended to be too stupid to learn. I thought she would give up after a couple of weeks, but she knew that I needed to do those dishes more than those dishes needed to be done. When my mother would not give up on me, I realized that there was no escape from the dishes, and that if I said for the next ten years that I did not know how to wash them, then for the next ten years my mother would daily teach me how to do them.

I hear many parents complaining about the kind of music their children like. I am told that many of the new rock records have sexually explicit lyrics and tend to glorify what is evil and ugly. Yet, in most cases, teenagers get into an undiscriminating style of listening to rock music because their parents are too lazy to do anything about it. Sloth is responsible for parents allowing their children to go off to their rooms, shut their doors and listen to the latest recordings of Prince or Black Sabbath. It is laziness on the part of parents which is responsible for their laissez-faire attitude toward the development of their children's taste in music.

To ask what records are being purchased, to ask about the messages of the songs and to discuss the value of the music with their children requires more time and effort than most parents are willing to expend. Thus, a generation is left to the corrupting influence of a rock subculture because so many parents are unwilling to address the hard task of training their teenagers. It is true that parental control can become too restrictive. However, in most cases, the problems of youth are not related to parents demanding too much of them, but rather, demanding too little, because they are slothful.

I do not mean to suggest that if parents work as hard as they should at disciplining their children, all will be ideal. It should be noted that God had two perfect children, Adam and Eve, whom He reared in the perfect environment of Eden; yet both of them rebelled against His will. Where there is freedom there will be rebellion; still, parents should imitate the Heavenly Father, and never give up on their children. God works hard at being our Father and we should work hard at being parents to our children.

TOO LAZY TO ENJOY

Joy in Christ requires a commitment to working at the Christian lifestyle. Salvation comes as a gift, but the joy of salvation demands disciplined action. Most Christians I know have just enough of the Gospel to make them miserable, but not enough to make them joyful. They know enough about the biblical message to keep them from doing those things which the world tempts them to do; but they do not have enough of a commitment to God to do those things through which they might experience the fullness of His joy.

I know of a young woman who lacked any semblance of joy in her life, even though she had accepted Christ as her Saviour. She lived a life of relative piety and went to church on Sundays with fair regularity. Nevertheless, life was depressing for her and she seemed bored with it. She went to a Christian psychotherapist for help, but after several sessions with him, felt that the effort was futile. Then one day she came into her therapist's office with her face radiant with excitement "I've had the most wonderful day," she said. "This morning I could not get my car started, so I called the pastor and asked him if he could drive me to my appointment with you. He said he would, but on the way he had to stop by the hospital and make a few calls. I went with him and while I was in the hospital, I visited some elderly people in one of the wards. I read from the Bible and prayed with them. By the time the morning was over, I was higher than a kite. I haven't felt this good in years."

The psychotherapist quickly responded, "Now we know how to make you happy! Our problem is solved! Now we know to keep you out of the doldrums!"

Much to his surprise, the young woman answered, "You don't expect me to do this sort of thing every day, do you?"

Here is a very specific case in which the person knew what she had to do to experience joy, but was too lazy to do it. Sloth takes away the possibility of joy. Those who are not happy should make a list of those things they know God wants changed in their lives. Then, asking the Lord to help them, they should set out to bring about those changes. Those who allow God to have His way with them will find their lives infused with the joy and peace they seek.

Unfortunately, the tendency to be controlled by sloth kills the desire to change for the better. Sloth is a condition of the heart which works against doing what is necessary to find joy in life or to experience salvation. Most people know they need to be saved sometime and think that they may get around to putting things right with God some day, but they lack motivation to get moving on it now. Sloth takes a terrible toll.

TOO LAZY TO BECOME

Some people are afraid of becoming Christians because they know that there are changes they will have to make, and are unwilling to do so. They want cheap grace that requires little response to what Jesus has done for them. They do not accept the fact that the good works God desires of them are means through which their joy might become full. They are afraid to become what God believes that they can be, because they are too lazy to face the challenges of living out the will of God in their daily activities.

It is possible in any church to find people who want to be a part of the group, not because they find that the orthodox positions of Christianity are true, but because they do *not* want to think and work out the meaning of the Bible through honest labor. They find it easier to believe things to be true because some authoritarian person declares them to be true. They accept what they are taught without evaluation or question. It is work to search the Scriptures in order to determine whether or not what is being taught is biblical.

It is hard to struggle with working out the relationship of salvation to the affairs of everyday life. It is easier to let some "authority" tell us how to live and to explain what the Bible requires of us. The lazy like to be delivered from the arduous tasks associated with thinking about the meaning of Scripture for their lives and the painful process of changing their lifestyles.

When I was in the eighth grade, my math teacher gave our class a textbook which had the answers to the problems in the back of the book. She told us not to use those answers, but to work the problems out for ourselves. Most of us in the class could not resist the temptation to peep at those answers as we did our homework. We found it so much easier to "work out" the assigned problems if we had the answers in advance. However, those of us who took this easy route with our homework usually flunked the tests. I am convinced that the same is true in the Christian life. Those who try to get by on the answers of others probably will be unprepared for the real tests of life. Each of us should struggle with what we have been taught through Scripture and work out the meaning of these teachings for our everyday lives so that we can be certain of the faith that lies within us.

The church too often provides a haven for the slothful, especially if leaders want unquestioning acceptance of what they preach. Christians need to be encouraged to work out their own salvation with fear and trembling (Phil. 2:12). They need to avoid tendencies to sloth in their lives. Growing up in Christ is hard work, and other people cannot do it for us. We are called to do those things that will foster spiritual maturity.

A STYLE OF PROCRASTINATION

Parents know that one of the most effective techniques children use to get out of assigned work is to promise to do it later. Procrastination is an effective tool for the slothful. They can make themselves appear responsible even though they do nothing. The slothful hope that if they put off their work long enough, they can somehow escape from it.

Lazy college students usually put off reading the assigned textbook material until the night before the final examination, and usually fail to do research papers until the night before they are due. Procrastination is the most common the cause of academic failure in higher education.

On several occasions, I have run out of gas because I did not feel like going to get the tank filled up. Somehow I felt that a later time would be better and, in each case, I suffered unnecessarily for not doing what I should have done.

Procrastination is one of the most effective weapons in Satan's arsenal. It is impossible to estimate the number of people who intended to become Christians at some later time, but who were not willing to make the decision when they were confronted with the Gospel. King Agrippa responded to the convicting message of the Apostle Paul by saying: "Almost thou persuadest me to be a Christian!" (Acts 26:28, KJV) Sloth causes us to put off until tomorrow what is not absolutely required today. Agrippa put off making a decision for Christ and probably never did get around to doing what he was almost persuaded to do after hearing Paul's defense.

I remember attending revival meetings as a boy in which "Almost Persuaded" was used as a closing hymn:

> "Almost persuaded, now to believe;
> Almost persuaded, Christ to receive;"
> Seems now some soul to say,
> "Go, Spirit, go Thy way,
> Some more convenient day
> On Thee I'll call."

The Bible always calls us to act in the present. The Old Testament leader cried out:

> "Choose this day whom ye will serve; whether the gods which your fathers served that were on the other side of the flood, or the gods of the Amorites, in whose land ye dwell; but as for me and my house, we will serve the Lord" (Josh. 24:15, KJV).

In the New Testament we are told: "Behold, now is the acceptable time; behold now is the day of salvation" (2 Cor. 6:2). Those who are lazy can always find some reason for delaying action, hoping that if they delay long enough, they will not have to act at all. Usually, they procrastinate until it is too late to act.

There are many parents who know that they should take time to share the Gospel with their children. They know that they ought to instruct their children in biblical teachings and that they ought to lead their children in family worship. They know what they ought to do, but they suffer from inertia. When their children assume a course of action that is destructive and sinful, they cry out, "If only I had done what I was supposed to do as a parent, this would not have happened." Procrastinating parents may hope subconsciously that even if they do not share the teachings of the Bible with their children, others will. They often realize too late that their children have failed to receive what they should have in Christian instruction. In the words of the nineteenth-century American poet, John Greenleaf Whittier:

> For all sad words of tongue or pen,
> The saddest are these: "It might have been!"

I am convinced that on Judgment Day, the sins of omission will loom larger than the sins of commission. Consequently, more sins will have resulted from sloth than from all the other sins put together. In his letter to the church at Ephesus, Paul writes: "Look carefully then how you walk, not as unwise men but as wise, making the most of the time, because the days are evil" (Eph. 5:15-16). His admonition carries significant implications for all Christians. It is important to think of what can be done for Christ at home or at work, to consider ways to contribute to the well-being of others, to strive to become all that we can become as we do those things which God has called us to do. It is tragic to let opportunities of the moment slip away because of sloth, to allow life to be consumed in laziness. It is vital to respond to the challenges that each day presents.

One day a middle-aged man came to my office to talk with me. He explained how he had let the opportunity to serve God in a heroic and magnificent manner slip away from him. He told me, "Doc, once I was going to be a missionary and do something important for the kingdom of God, but I didn't do it. I kept putting off taking the necessary steps that would enable me to fulfill the will of God for my life. Now it's too late. My time has passed. There's no way I can ever do what will please God. I'm married and have two kids in college. I'm in debt up to my ears. There's no way I can stop everything in order to take up the call to Christian service. I came to urge you to talk to your students and to keep them from making the same mistake I made. Keep them from putting off serving Jesus until it's too late."

I almost lost my temper with him. "Look," I said, "I don't want to hear about what you might have done for Jesus twenty years ago. I want to talk about what you are going to do for Him today. I think you're using the failures of the past to evade the challenges of the present. You're still excusing yourself from the tasks which God has set before you. Only now you're trying to make your present responsibilities seem unimportant compared to what you think you should have done twenty years ago."

The man was shaken by what I laid on him, and that allowed me the opportunity to go on. "You may think that the *little* things you can do for the Lord now are relatively unimportant, but the Bible says that if we are faithful in a very little things, we shall have authority over great things. Why not get on with doing the work of God that is waiting to be done right now?"

GETTING RID OF SLOTH

The way to be rid of sloth is to become subject to the Holy Spirit. The same Jesus, who died 2,000 years ago on the cross to atone for our sins, is resurrected and present with us now through His Holy Spirit. All of us who believe in what Jesus did for us then are able to invite the Holy Spirit to effect changes in our lives here and now.

In the Epistle to the Romans, the Apostle Paul explains some of the changes that the Holy Spirit will bring about in our lives if we want Him to: "If the Spirit of Him who raised Jesus from the dead dwells in you, He who raised Christ Jesus from the dead will give life to your mortal bodies also through the Spirit which dwells in you" (Rom. 8:11).

• The life generated by the Holy Spirit displaces the deadness that seems to typify those who are subject to the demonic influence of sloth. Laziness saps the vitality out of human existence. All of us who have wasted time know of that debilitation.

Days spent watching soap operas on television do not invigorate us. Rather, they leave us with a psychological fatigue. Sloth does not create a sense of well-being, but leaves us dissipated and groggy. However, when we open ourselves up to the Holy Spirit, He "quickens" us. Just as new life was imparted to the corpse of Jesus, giving Him the ability to rise from the dead, even so the Holy Spirit will give life to those who are deadened by sloth. Our repentance from sin and inward surrender to the will of God makes us fertile soil for the fruit of the Spirit to take root and grow, driving the deadness of our souls away.

• Also, surrender to the Holy Spirit gives us a sense of direction as to what we should do. The Spirit thus enables us to overcome one of the major contributors to inaction and sloth—indecision. Without a sense of direction, we often find ourselves paralyzed by inability to decide what we ought to do. The Spirit of God delivers us from such a state of ambiguity by helping us to discern what we ought to be doing with our lives.

A young woman who was a student of mine at Eastern College seemed unable to generate any enthusiasm for studying. Her grades were poor and her attitude toward her work was extremely negative. She was a classic example of sloth. She was continually late for class, and often cut. I could count on her drifting off to sleep during the lecture on those days when she favored us with her presence.

Halfway through her first semester at college, she became friends with a vivacious Christian who was a dynamic leader in the Youth For Christ movement. Her new friend took an intense interest in her and, over the course of a few weeks, led her into a conversion experience that transformed her into a vital Christian. Overnight her academic performance changed. She was alert in class. Her assignments were done with care and insight. Her interest in the subject matter would have delighted any teacher. When I asked her about the dramatic change in her attitude, she explained to me that since she had accepted Christ, she had gained direction and purpose for her life. She claimed that she sensed that God was leading her into Christian service and that this gave her academic program new meaning. She didn't mind working, because she knew what she was working for

God provides a purpose for life. He convinces those who surrender to the work of the Holy Spirit in their lives that they are called to be on mission in His name. When such a sense of divine calling is imparted to people, they inevitably respond with enthusiasm and are freed from the burden of sloth.

● Fear of failure is a major contributor to laziness. The Apostle Paul tells us: "For you did not receive the spirit of slavery to fall back into fear, but you have received the spirit of sonship" (Rom. 8:15). This is good news to those of us who have found our lives frozen in sloth because we were afraid to act. If we are afraid that our efforts will come to nothing, and that we will appear ludicrous for attempting what we cannot do, we will probably attempt very little.

It is hard to say what percentage of children do poorly in school because they do not try, but I believe that many do not try because they are afraid of failure. These children often do not attempt to do their assignments because they know that if they do not try, they can still maintain the image of being intelligent. However, if they try and fail, they will be exposed as the inferior persons they believe themselves to be. Sloth is nurtured by fear. As long as children can convince the significant others in their lives that they are failing because they are not trying, they do not run the risk of failing because they are inadequate.

All of this changes when persons surrender their lives to the will of God and allow God to impart His Spirit to them. In Romans 8:16-17, we read: "It is the Spirit Himself bearing witness to our spirit that we are the children of God, and if children then heirs, heirs of God and fellow heirs with Christ, provided we suffer with Him in order that we may also be glorified with Him."

Feelings of inferiority will be eliminated in those who are inwardly convinced by the Holy Spirit that they are children and heirs of God, and that they will be glorified with Christ forever. The new status imparted to Spirit-filled Christians will create a confidence and self-assurance that will encourage them to attempt things they hitherto considered impossible. Their relationship with God through the infilling of the Spirit transforms them into fearless doers of those things they believe God wants them to do. Their new self-confidence overcomes the fears generated by former feelings of inferiority.

This self-confidence is the result of their new concept of themselves as sons and daughters of God. The immobility of sloth is abolished and they are willing to give each task their best efforts, not worrying about the consequences. They know that if they faithfully do the will of God, the results need not be of concern to them. God has called them to be faithful rather than to be successful. They are assured that "in everything God works for good with those who love Him, who are called according to His purpose" (Rom. 8:28).

● Lastly, the Holy Spirit motivates us out of a slothful state of consciousness because a needy world is waiting for us to become what we should be and do what we should do. "For the creation waits with eager longing for the revealing of the sons of God" (Rom. 8:19).

When the Holy Spirit fills us, we begin to feel what Jesus feels for His fallen creation. There are injustices, corrupt social practices, arms races, and wars. Economic oppression, hunger, and racial discrimination seem universal. Truly all of creation is in desperate need of the transforming efforts of a people led and empowered by God. The work of the Holy Spirit in our lives is not intended only to perfect us so that we will be fit for heaven when we die, but to equip us to be God's agents for change in this present age. The Spirit imparts to us the passion of Christ's mission which He Himself set forth:

> "The Spirit of the Lord is upon Me, because He hath anointed Me to preach the Gospel to the poor; He hath sent Me to heal the brokenhearted, to preach deliverance to the captives, and recovering of sight to the blind, to set at liberty them that are bruised, to preach the acceptable year of the Lord" (Luke 4:18-19, KJV).

To be filled with the Spirit is to have our hearts broken by the things that break the heart of Jesus. To be alive in the Spirit is to view people through the eyes of Christ. Consequently, whenever we see anyone suffering, we will feel what Christ feels for that person and seek to alleviate that suffering. Whenever we see anyone hungry, we will view that person as Jesus does and seek to feed that person. Whenever we see someone imprisoned, we will long to see that captive set free because we desire what Christ wills for that person. Being filled with the Spirit creates within us a hunger for justice and a craving for the salvation of the lost. With such an orientation to the world, it is impossible to maintain a slothful attitude.

Sloth deadens, but the Spirit gives life. Sloth thrives on feelings of inferiority, but the Spirit gives us the assurance that we are the children of God. Sloth is self-centered, but the Spirit creates a burning desire to change the world. Sloth leaves us bored and empty, but in the Spirit we find the fullness of God's joy.

*There are some slight differences of opinion as to which sins should be included in this list of deadly sins and some discussion as to the order in which they should be listed. At least three different versions of the list have come down to us through history. The selection of the list of sins given here is, so far as I could ascertain, the one most commonly accepted. Furthermore, after careful consideration I believe that the given order of the list best suggests the hierarchy of their relative importance.

CHAPTER TWO
LUST

SIGMUND FREUD shocked the Victorian world by declaring that sex was a preoccupation of all human beings. His comprehensive study of human nature and his analysis of human behavior led him to conclude that all of life is permeated with a craving for sexual gratification. According to Freud, even religious experience was filled with sexual overtones and meanings. When, as a young graduate student, I first read Freud, I dismissed his theories as totally devoid of truth. I refused to accept his premises and certainly disagreed with his conclusions. However, I have come to believe that this founder of modern psychotherapy cannot be dismissed so easily. This cynical explorer of human motivations makes more sense of what people think and do than most of us are willing to admit on reading his work for the first time.

The Apostle Paul probably would have found much in Freud's opinions with which he could have agreed. Paul, like Freud, understood lust to be a repressed, illicit sexual desire, which is a normal part of every human psyche. Paul made clear in his epistles that before the transforming power of Christ comes into our lives, we are people who are controlled by the lusts of the flesh. "For the flesh lusteth against the Spirit, and the Spirit against the flesh; and these are contrary the one to the other, so that ye cannot do the things that ye would" (Gal. 5:17, KJV). As a consequence of being fallen creatures, we have a natural tendency toward sexual perversion:

Wherefore God also gave them up to uncleanness through the lusts of their own hearts, to dishonor their own bodies between themselves; who changed the truth of God into a lie, and worshiped and served the creature more than the Creator, who is blessed forever. Amen.

For this cause God gave them up unto vile affections; for even their women did change the natural use into that which is against nature; and likewise also the men, leaving the natural use of the woman, burned in their lust one toward another; men with men working that which is unseemly, and receiving in themselves that recompence of their error which was meet (Rom. 1:24-27, KJV).

According to Paul, lust is a perversion of love. Lust is the result of a demonic twisting of love. When we are converted by the Holy Spirit, we will be restored to what we were meant to be, and only then will we be motivated by love.

It is clear in Paul's writings that the primary thing that differentiates the behavior of the new person in Christ from the unconverted person is that the new person lives life to express love while the old person lived life to fulfill lust.

This simple dichotomy separating the love-motivated Christian from the lust-motivated person could lead many of us to doubt our salvation. Paul's differentiation between these two types of people seems so crisply clear that when we experience lust, we may take the experience as evidence that we are not Christians. It is easy to conclude from Pauline writings that lust is the litmus test that designates us as unregenerate types who are alienated from God and devoid of the Holy Spirit. Not only does Paul offer us a clear-cut division of humanity into one group made up of love-motivated Christians and another group made up of lust-motivated sinners, but John and James support his judgment. Added to the spiritual self-doubt that is generated by these apostolic writings are the words of Jesus, who tells us: "You have heard it said, 'You shall not commit adultery.' But I say to you that every one who looks at a woman lustfully has already committed adultery with her in his heart."

When new Christians read passages such as these, they sometimes are driven to despair. It would be easy for a newly converted person to reason, "Christians are delivered from lust and do not even think lustful thoughts. But I still have lustful cravings and I still harbor lustful thoughts. Therefore, I must not be a Christian." The problem is made worse by the fact that there are always some church members around who claim to have reached a state of sinless perfection in which they no longer have any lustful dimensions to their personalities.

The Apostle Paul recognized this tendency to despair among sincere Christians who, in spite of accepting Christ as Lord, still experienced lust in their lives. His response to those who taught that the saved are spiritually perfected is brilliantly set forth in his Epistle to the Philippians. There were pious pretenders in the Philippian church who put down those who, in humble honesty, admitted to having sin in their hearts. Paul endeavored to set the record straight on this issue.

> Not as though I had already attained, either were already perfect; but I follow after, if that I may apprehend that for which also I am apprehended of Christ Jesus. Brethren, I count not myself to have apprehended; but this one thing I do, forgetting those things which are behind, and reaching forth unto those things which are before, I press towrd the mark for the prize of the high calling of God in Christ Jesus (Phil. 3:12-14, KJV).

In this passage Paul makes it clear that as a Christian, he was a person who was "in process." He declared that the Spirit did not instantaneously transform him into a perfected person; because there was much within him that warred against the work of the Spirit. In the Epistle to the Romans, he wrote:

> For I delight in the Law of God, in my inmost self, but I see in my members another law at war with the law of my mind and making me captive to the law of sin which dwells in my members. Wretched man that I am! Who will deliver me from this body of death? (Rom. 7:22-24)

When we become Christians, we give to the Holy Spirit the freedom to transform us into new creatures who are freed from sin and motivated by love. However, this transformation takes time. The lusts of the flesh must be driven out of our consciousness, and that process takes a lifetime to complete. If we are spiritually disciplined through regular prayer, Bible study and the strengthening fellowship of other Christians, we can experience increasing conquest over the flesh by the Spirit. There will be struggles and temporary setbacks, but in the midst of all this Paul gives us this assurance.

> We are afflicted in every way, but not crushed; perplexed, but not driven to despair; persecuted, but not forsaken; struck down, but not destroyed; always carrying in the body the death of Jesus, so that the life of Jesus may also be manifested in our bodies (2 Cor. 4:8-10).

When I say that it will take more than a lifetime to be freed from all the effects of the lusts of the flesh, I do so in the confidence that beyond the grave we will become people who are fully motivated by love as God intends us to be. Jude 24 tells us that when the Spirit finishes His work in us, He will be able joyfully to present us "faultless" before the throne of grace. And the Apostle John gives us the good news that when we see Christ, either on His return or in the resurrection, we shall be as pure as Jesus Himself (1 John 3:2).

WHILE YOU'RE WAITING
FOR THE SECOND COMING

Having faced the realistic declaration of Scripture that freedom from lust is not something which is instantaneously experienced with conversion, but is the result of a long and arduous spiritual struggle, we must press on toward becoming what Christ expects us to become. In order to do this we must carefully examine those things which increase lust, so that we may avoid them, and discover those things which enhance love, so that we can develop them in our lives.

I have already stated that lust is a perversion of love. In the famous narrative poem *Don Juan* by Lord Byron, we read of a man who seeks psychological gratification through sexual escapades. Don Juan looks for a woman who will meet *his* needs and satisfy *his* appetites. If the libertine of our day regards Don Juan as an ideal type to be imitated, as he seduces woman after woman, he misses the whole point of the story. Don Juan is a tragic figure who hungers for something that he never seems to experience. He longs for an erotic turn-on which will leave him not only physically satiated but psychically fulfilled. Don Juan seeks that woman who will make him fully alive and emotionally ecstatic. Like the worshipers of Dionysius in the ancient Greek world, Don Juan hopes for a sexual experience which will fill the spiritual vacuum of his soul. His tragedy is inevitable because lust does not deliver what it seems to promise. The gratification sought through sexual conquests is never delivered. Don Juan, like the rest of us, is deluded into thinking that the living out of sexual fantasies can give unspeakable joy.

Most of us have fantasized sexual experiences. The only difference between us and Don Juan is that he lived out his fantasies, while we usually do not, often more because we lack opportunity or audacity rather than because we are spiritual.

There was a time when I would have pretended that such was not the case. I was sure that the other Christians I knew would be shocked and break fellowship with me if they knew what went on in my mind. Those in the church seemed beyond the lustful fantasies which plagued my consciousness. However, I have since learned that I am not the only one in the church who, from time to time, fantasizes about the possible joys of sexual liasons. In the words of one preacher: "It's depressing to realize that most of us are like the rest of us." The problem we have with lust is common to all who live this side of Eden.

What we all must learn is that lust does not deliver what it promises. If we were to live out our fantasies, we would not experience psychic ecstasy; instead we would experience the filthy side of personhood in a heightened sense. Soren Kierkegaard, having lived out one of his sexual fantasies by visiting a house of prostitution, wrote in his diary: "Tonight I paid a woman in order to experience my own despicableness." It may be true that at the moment of sexual satisfaction the person motivated by lust feels transported into a state of bliss; but that brief moment is quickly followed by a sense of emptiness and shame.

Erich Fromm, a disciple of Freud, understood this truth and broke ranks with his academic mentor primarily because he recognized that Freud failed to grasp the real hunger of human personality. According to Fromm, all of us have been created to gain our ultimate fulfillment in life from loving, rather than through the gratification of our sexual appetites. This world-famous neo-Freudian humanist is correct when he declares that lust creates a desire to gain through sex with the partners of our fantasies what can only be gained through loving self-giving.

The Apostle Paul wrote to the Roman Christians about the delusions of thinking that sex will provide our richest satisfactions. He described in graphic detail how the failure to gain the expected gratification will drive us to more and more extreme perversity as we hope that in some stranger and more estoeric sexual experience, we will find what has eluded us in our earlier sexual experiences. Lust leads us to extreme degradation as we seek to gain a sense of fulfillment by living out the fantasies which it generates. Paul further explained that lust drives people into such things as witchcraft. A study of Satan worship will reveal that in most cases, people get into it as a make-believe ritual that is part of perverted sexual games. Only later do they begin to view their satanic worship as a religious experience.

Some years ago, a foreign film captured the attention of students of the cinema. The film, *La Dolce Vita,* picked up the theme of the gradual denigration of a modern man living in the sophisticated circles of Roman society, as he continually sought new ways to satisfy his sexual appetite. The film traced his decline into the occult, step by step, as he moved from one kind of sexual practice to another. In his moral collapse, he sought ever new forms of stimulation as the practices already tried lost their ability to excite him. Throughout his descent into the depths of demonic corruption, there were constant appeals from those who represented purity and love, but his lust controlled him and eventually led him into a pit of filth and degradation.

LUST AS ILLUSION

Perhaps the most deceptive aspect of lust is that the more a person tries to satisfy it, the more intense it becomes. To feed lust is to generate an even greater hunger for its gratification. The person who yields to lust finds that the more the lust of the flesh is fed, the more ravishing it becomes. In short, when it comes to sexual lust, the more one gets, the less one is satisfied. It is this desperate longing created by yielding to lust that drives the individual into the hands of the demonic.

The longing to satisfy sexual lusts becomes so strong that one is willing to call upon the powers of darkness in the hope that the hungers of the flesh might be satiated. The ultimate tragedy is that the Evil One is the great deceiver and gives what people *think* they crave, only to leave them emotionally empty and spiritually unfulfilled. Satan mocks those who worship him by delivering what they want while denying what they really need. Lust is his ultimate weapon in the battle for souls.

Lust is an illusion, but love never fails. As Paul said, in 1 Corinthians 13:8, "Love never ends; as for prophecies, they will pass away; as for tongues, they will cease; as for knowledge, it will pass away." It is ironic that setting aside the desire for one's own gratification, and seeking to bring joy and fulfillment into the lives of others, provides the psychic gratification that eludes those who seek it through lust.

I saw Mother Teresa just once, but in that brief encounter I recognized in her a deep joy and serenity. She does not seek joy for herself, nor does she make self-actualization a quest of her life; nevertheless, she has found both. She realizes that the joy for which the heart longs cannot be gained by seeking for it, but comes unexpectedly to those who lovingly sacrifice themselves and all that they possess for the sake of the joy of others. It is this lesson that we learn from Christ's words: "If any man will come after Me, let him deny himself and take up his cross, and follow Me. For whoever would save his life will lose it, and whoever loses his life for My sake will find it" (Matt. 16:24-25).

In order to illustrate this biblical truth I want to contrast two marriages. In the first marriage, the husband complains constantly that his wife does not gratify a vast array of his psychic/sexual needs. He is planning to leave her and take up with another woman who "really turns me on." "Hey," he says, "it's not my fault that she fails to gratify me. We can't change the way we are."

This husband portrays the selfishness of so many who enter into marriage with the expectation that their partners are obligated to meet their needs. Blinded by the pop psychology outlined in some of today's bestsellers, they think that marriage is an arrangement designed to deliver physical and emotional delights and actualize all their potentialities for happiness. These children of the cult of romanticism have bought into the lyrics of the songs that lead our hit parade and tell us such things as: "Lay Your Hands on Me," "I Miss You, Can't Stand to Live Without You," "Talk to Me, Me, Me," "Fairy Tale Lovers," and "Lost Without Your Love."

The self-centeredness of much of our romanticism is often ignored, but anyone who carefully examines the expectations that people usually bring to marriages will discover that most of them seek their own gratification without realizing that such an orientation has nothing to do with love. In the words of the Apostle Paul in 1 Corinthians 13:5, love is "not arrogant or rude. Love does not insist on its own way; it is not irritable or resentful."

In the second marriage, the husband is committed to his wife's happiness. Every day he tries to think of something he can do that will give her joy. I got to know this man because he brought his wife to me for vocational counseling. She had some writing ability and he wanted to know if it was possible for her to enroll in a journalism program at our college. Though her husband had not had the opportunity for a college education, he was excited about the prospect for his wife. He promised that if the college would take her as a student, she would have plenty of time for study because he would do the housework. When I asked him if it bothered him that his wife would be better educated than he was, I realized that he had never thought about it. All that he wanted was for his wife to have the opportunity to fulfill her dream to be a writer and to that end he was willing to make any sacrifice. I have seldom met anyone as thrilled about life as that man was, or, in the terminology of Abraham Maslow, more self-actualized. Love meets our needs; lust delivers a void.

Those who complain that this biblical prescription for life

ignores the sexual needs of people, belong to what James H.S. Bussard, one of my graduate school professors at the University of Pennsylvania, mockingly called, "The pure orgasm school of thought." Bossard claimed that those who think that the "right" partners and the "right" techniques will produce marital bliss are greatly mistaken. According to his observations, those who paid little attention to things like sexual adjustment, but concentrated on making each other happy, proved to be the most sexually fulfilled persons he knew. I concur with Bossard and claim that lust betrays; as we live out the fantasies which lust generates, we gain little satisfaction in bed or, for that matter, in life. On the other hand, if we love our marital partners and sacrifice for *their* happiness and fulfillment, our marriages will deliver more joy than we ever could have imagined and more sexual pleasure than those who live by lust ever could dream possible

LUST AS IMMATURITY

In 1 Corinthians 13, often called the Love Chapter of the Bible, the Apostle Paul points out that love is mature. He declares that there comes a time when our childish emotions must be outgrown because we are required to live like adults. Paul wrote in verse 11: "When I was a child, I spake as a child, I understood as a child, I thought as a child; but when I became a man, I put away childish things" (KJV)

Lust is a childish thing. This is particularly evident as it expresses itself in the lives of married people. A young woman I knew enjoyed having an array of men want her as a partner. She dated many and was considered a femme fatale who could have any man she wanted. She eventually married, but in her marital state could not find contentment with one man; she wanted them all.

The inability to make choices is a primary mark of immaturity. I can remember when I was a boy going to the store with a quarter in my hand, and having the delightful opportunity to buy some candy. I remember standing in front of the candy counter for what must have seemed forever to the clerk, trying to decide which kind of candy I should choose. There were so many different kinds that I would find myself immobilized.

When the impatience of the clerk finally would force me to decide, I would be filled with anxiety, and as soon as I had made my selection, I would wish for another kind of candy, which suddenly seemed much more appealing than what I had in my hand.

Being unable to choose one of a variety of possible delights is cute behavior for a ten-year-old, but is unbefitting a person of thirty-five. By that age people should have the courage to make decisions and then to believe that what they have decided is the most glorious of all the choices that could have been made. To make a choice and then vacillate and yearn for something else is childish.

At an office party, a junior executive began to "make moves" on one of the secretaries. After several of his clumsy come-ons, I overheard the young woman say with a tone of irritation in her voice, "Bill, why don't you grow up and go home to your wife?"

"What a fitting response," I thought. That was exactly what was wrong with that man—he needed to grow up. He had chosen a woman for his wife, and still wanted her; but he wanted other women too. In his immaturity, he refused to accept the limitations which his decision had imposed on him. He did not recognize that maturity involves a willingness to accept the limitations that go with choices and an ability to find joy in the situation one has chosen.

Lust thrives on immaturity. It encourages the imagination to fantasize about what it would be like to have this partner or that partner in bed. It gets people to play foolish games in which they try to hold on to the sexual partner they have chosen while at the same time trying to seduce for their own pleasure others whom they are forbidden to possess. But Scripture teaches that one should "put away childish things," or, to put it more bluntly, to grow up!

Maturity is not passive resignation to the inevitable, but rather the state of mind that enables persons to create magnificent possibilities for happiness in the situations in which they find themselves. Abraham Lincoln once said, "Most folks are about as happy as they make up their minds to be." That makes sense. In most cases, persons who are sexually fulfilled in their marriages are that way because, having made a decision to be married, they simultaneously made a decision to find sexual fulfillment with their mates. On the other hand, much sexual dissatisfaction in marriage stems from the fact that people refuse to take full advantage of the possibilities for sexual gratification that are inherent in their marriages. Refusing to live within the limitations imposed by their marriages, they lust after other possibilities. If such childish persons do get out of their marriages and into the relationships about which they have fantasized, they undoubtedly will be disappointed. Their lustful cravings will not be gratified with their new partners, no matter what they dream, because their own failure to be satisfied with what they have is the real cause of their joylessness. Like little children, they do not want what they possess, regardless of how wonderful it is; but instead, long for what they are not allowed to have. The immature, who do not glory in what is theirs to enjoy, are easy victims of lust.

LUST AS A DENIAL OF DEATH

One of Freud's most brilliant contemporary interpreters, Ernest Becker, in his Pulitzer Prize winning book, *Denial of Death*, contends that throughout our lives a growing consciousness of our own mortality is an increasingly dominant factor in our behavior. Becker helps us to see that most of what we do, and especially our sexual behavior, is the result of our vain attempt to suppress the intolerable awareness that we are moving inexorably toward death. Our bodies constantly provide reminders that we are getting older. Who among us middle-aged citizens has not stood pensively in front of a mirror and viewed with dismay what is, while remembering what has been lost?

Our thighs have become flabby and our hair (if there is any) loses its lustre. Cosmetics can do only so much for biological clocks that are winding down. In the midst of the malaise brought on by encroaching death, we look for deliverance. Usually we do not care from whence the deliverance comes, as long as it provides an escape from the pain of knowing what is happening to us. We will accept all forms of lies and distractions if they can make us forget the sinking feeling in the depths of our souls. Such is the fertile soil in which lust can be planted and thrive.

The lusts of the flesh seem to offer a diversion, causing us to forget that we are dying. They promise relief from the emptiness that comes with our knowledge of the inevitability of death. The imagined joy of being transported from the mundane by forbidden sexual pleasures seems like a way of salvation to our lost souls.

Who among us does not know of some person who had position, wealth, and family and then threw them all aside to fulfill a craving of the flesh? Which one of us has not thought of risking all that we hold dear in order to enjoy a moment of illicit pleasure? How often have we marveled at the scope of the disasters caused by yielding to sexual passions? David destroyed the glory of his kingdom in his lust for Bathsheba. Samson forfeited his charisma and strength for Delilah. Solomon allowed his wisdom to turn to cynicism because of his insatiable cravings for women. Who has not shuddered at what lust will drive people to do? Behind it all, contends Becker, is the desire to escape the consciousness of mortality.

The woman who is approaching menopause experiences a sense that her life is ending sooner than she thought it would. She becomes painfully aware that she is entering the waning years of her existence. The efforts of her husband to comfort her are of no avail; she realizes that she is losing more than her ability to bear children. She longs to express groanings which cannot be uttered. She wants to be young and attractive again. Then, unexpectedly, a man several years younger than she shows an interest in her. She wonders if, in spite of all that has happened to her over the years, she still possesses seductive powers. She asks herself if she appears to him younger than she really is. "Perhaps the aging process is not as obvious as I thought," she says to herself. "If I could just captivate him, then I would know." Then insidiously, lust begins to manifest itself. She imagines what it would be like to experience sexual ecstasy in his arms. And it is only a matter of time before she does. Her escape from reality happens without regard to the consequences.

There are few people I pity more than those middle-aged men trying to be "cool." With their slick casual shirts unbuttoned at the neck to display an array of gold chains, they attempt to look smooth and sophisticated. They try so hard to be men who know what life is all about as they hungrily eye the women. They fail to notice if their stomachs have swelled from drinking too much beer and their bellies hang over their belts. They try to conceal what is obvious to any objective observer; they are scared little men, pathetic parodies of the selves they would like to be. They look for some validation of the facade they project, and they think that it will come if they can just hustle some women. Any woman will do. They think to themselves, "I know I'm just as good in bed as I've ever been, maybe better." Lust is nurtured by their fears. They want sex for reasons that they themselves do not understand. The truth of why they lust is too painful for them to bear.

We cannot delude ourselves that all of this goes on only outside of the church. Many pastors have sought escape from their fears of death by way of excursions into sexual immorality. Their own sermons have made them more aware than most people of the transitory nature of life. The funerals and tragedies of others are part of a pastor's daily work and make the awareness of his/her own fraility all too real. It is difficult for any member of the clergy to be unaware of the presence of death in the midst of life. The laity is prone to assume that those in the pulpit live in the assurance of eternal life and therefore do not fear death. Many members would be shocked to learn of any self-doubt or lack of faith in eternal life in their clergy. Pastors are aware of this and respond by pretending that their steadfast convictions keep them from ever being troubled by such things. They learn to conceal their troubled souls within their clerical robes. But the fear of death is there, and the false affirmation of life through lust is a real danger.

I tremble at the thought of pastors counseling women in one-to-one situations. Very often such counseling sessions are difficult to handle because they encourage a level of honesty and reciprocity in which the counselor is often confessing to the counselee. Then there are two desperate souls reaching out to each other for affirmation. At first it is just an affectionate embrace. . . . simply an expression of Christian love. Later there comes more . . . and still later. . . . Hurting people are vulnerable. Spiritual counseling intensifies the consciousness of hurt and makes people seek comfort and escape without thinking rationally about the consequences. Lust lurks in the shadows of our minds waiting to express itself whenever fears about death and about the meaninglessness of life are exposed.

At a recent meeting of psychotherapists, a survey of participants revealed that a majority of them at one time or another had experienced sexual relations with their clients. While I am sure that the percentage of pastors who have such experiences would be significantly lower, I am also sure that the realities would be shocking. Because of the vulnerability to sexual exploitation that exists in counseling situations, extreme care must be exercised. Ideally, counseling should occur between members of the same sex. The next best arrangement is for a pastor to have his wife present when he counsels members of the opposite sex. Finally, if counseling must take place cross-sexually without others being present, it should be in a setting that is open and visible. To counsel behind closed doors is asking for trouble. Some of my more sophisticated colleagues in the counseling business will disagree with this advice. They will say that I fear that lust is lurking in every consciousness and that people will be tempted to give vent to their lusts whenever opportunity presents itself. In response I must say that it is much better to be safe than sorry. Too many ministries have been left in ruins and too many people have been hurt because insufficient care was exercised as to where and with whom counseling was undertaken.

THE INSIGHTS OF FEMINISTS

It is amazing to me to witness so much wholesale condemnation of the insights of feminist leaders on the part of some who speak for evangelical Christianity. The truth is that much of what the feminists are saying needs to be heard by Christians, especially in male-dominated churches.

Often the most meaningful insights into the nature of lust, and the most intense condemnations of lust come from the feminist movement. This is easy to understand, since women are more likely to be victimized by lust than are men. Over the years, women have lost their reputations as men have laughingly "sown their wild oats." Women have been the victims of sexual exploitation and rape. They are the ones who suffer most from the sins of the flesh.

There are those who argue that it takes two to have sex and that the man and woman are equally to blame. At first that argument seems viable, but careful sociological studies will poke holes in it. In-depth interviews have revealed that men and women relate to sex and love quite differently. Men find it easy and almost natural to separate love and sex. Consequently, it is very easy for them to have sexual affairs without much emotional involvement. Most women, on the other hand, have a strong tendency to link sex with love. When they have sexual affairs, they are usually more emotionally committed to their partners. This significant difference means that usually the sexual act is very meaningful to the woman, while the male partner has more interest in the physical gratification. While studies show that this differentiation between men and women is breaking down, demonstrating that it has cultural rather than biological roots, the differentiation still holds for most of the population.

In light of that differentiation, it is easy to see why women are more likely than men to be exploited because of lust. In another study it was revealed that while women most feared being used and then discarded, the greatest fear of men was failure.

A second reason for the condemnation of lust by feminists is their anger at being viewed as sex objects. They are angry with a society that expects women to have bodies shaped to stimulate the sexual desires of men. They rail against the cheerleaders at pro football games who serve no other purpose than to expose themselves to the lascivious ogling of the male spectators between plays of the game. They are tired of being evaluated for jobs on the basis of how they look instead of being judged by what they can do. They are irate over a tendency within our culture to make their primary raison d'etre to be sexually pleasing.

Is it any wonder that women with dignity reject such a function? Is it any surprise that they stand against a culture which would make them sexual things whose primary function is to serve as lust objects to a leering male population? Why does not the church join their crusade? Why is it that all that seems to concern us is the kind of pornography that reveals nudity, while we fail to recognize the kind of obscenity that reduces women to sexual "things"?

Many women suffer from the psychological oppression that comes with living in a sexist society. They are treated like sex objects and all too often are conditioned to enjoy this denigrating form of existence. There are many women who have learned to appreciate the sideward glances of men who mentally undress them. Such women thrive on the attention they get with their suggestive walks and poses, and, because they are winners at the game of "Who is the sexiest?" they are eager to play that game regardless of the costs. And the game *is* costly. The day always comes when those attributes that enabled them to win the game fade away. When that happens, such women are no longer of any value to the lustful watchers and, therefore, have little worth in their own eyes. Is it any wonder that the suicide rate for women over the age of thirty-five is disproportionately higher than for men over the same age?

Our Lord and Saviour Jesus Christ affirms the dignity of every person, male or female, in ways that transcend the standards of this lust-infected world. He lets us know that each of us is of worth to Him whose love has no limits and will never change. Jesus looks at us with love, never with lust. In His eyes we have everlasting value.

In Christ there is no sexism. As we grow into His likeness, we view others as He views them and hence we grow out of lust and look on others in love. As we are transformed by the Holy Spirit, we view ourselves differently. We are delivered from any false consciousness that leads us to see our worth in terms of how sexy we are, and we come to recognize that our worth is established by the fact that Christ loves each of us so much that He would have died for any one of us. In truth— He did.

HOW TO CONQUER LUST

The conquering of lust, as I stated earlier, is a lifelong process. However, it begins with a decision in the present. Having surrendered to the lordship of Christ, the Christian is expected to wish for the purification of the mind and heart. However, too many of us are like Saint Augustine, who once prayed, "O Lord, deliver me from lust—but not yet."

The Bible hits our problem sharply as it describes us as

people who love our sin (John 3:19-20). Lust gives us pleasure that we sometimes love more than we love Jesus. Consequently, the first step toward victory over lust is to wish to be free from its hold on us and to recognize that Jesus is willing and waiting to help us in this venture. Unfortunately, many of us have to wait until some dire consequence comes of our lust before we recognize our inability to overcome it by ourselves and call on Christ to undertake the struggle with us.

There was once a town reprobate who was wonderfully saved at a revival meeting. He pledged to start a new life and abandon his licentious ways, but he found that it was not easy to overcome the lusts of the flesh. Several months later he ran into the preacher who had led him to Christ and the preacher asked him directly, "Well, how's it been goin'?"

"It's been goin' awful," the convert responded. "It's like two teams of horse pullin' away at my soul. One team pullin' in one direction tryin' to get me to do what God wants and another team pullin' in the opposite direction tryin' to get me to do the things of the flesh."

"Let me ask you something," inquired the preacher. "Which team of horses wins?"

The new Christian answered with a twinkle in his eye, "Whichever team I says giddyup to."

In the end that's the position of each of us. God is able to help and He is willing to help—providing we want to change. The first step away from being controlled by lust is to wish to change by the grace of God.

The second step is to remember to think before you act. Remember what is at stake when you are tempted to give in to the lusts of the flesh. There is an old hymn of the church which says:

> I would be true, for there are those who trust me;
> I would be pure, for there are those who care;
> I would be strong, for there is much to suffer;
> I would be brave, for there is much to dare.

Some people suppose they can fulfill the lusts of the flesh without hurting anybody, because they think that nobody will ever find out about it. I am sure that there are those who do get away with it in this life, but I am equally convinced that there are more who are found out. In Arthur Miller's famous play, *Death of a Salesman,* Willy Loman, the main character, is in a hotel carrying on a dirty little affair with a woman he picked up in a bar. Much to his surprise, his son Biff comes to the hotel and happens on his father with this woman. In one moment, Biff's whole image of his father collapses, and from then on he sees his father as a cheap, pathetic person. Willy Loman never dreamed he would get caught, but he did, and then it was too late to make things right again. Willy could not help but ask, "Was it worth it?" The answer for Willy is the same as for all of us—"NO!" The risks are too great and the stakes are too high. Only a fool plays this game.

Even if we think we can fool all of the people all of the time, any kind of thoughtful reflection would lead to the conclusion that we can fool Jesus none of the time. He is always with us no matter where we are or what we do (Matt. 28:20). This truth which is our hope in times of trouble is also one we must remember when contemplating lust. The Apostle Paul reminds us that when we enter into illicit sexual acts, Jesus becomes a silent witness and a forced participant in what we do (1 Cor. 6:15). In the Book of Hebrews, we learn that being present in our degradation pains Him as much as the nails that pierced His hands and feet on the day of His crucifixion (Heb. 6:6).

ALTERNATIVES TO LUST

Sex should be fun. If Christian couples do not find fun and laughter in sex, they have perverted it. In the sexual act there should be superb enjoyment, and to make it less than that is to destroy its spirituality. The mistake of the Victorians was that they did not think that sex was good unless it was entered into with a somber disposition. The prevailing value system of the Victorians made women believe that sex was a painful ordeal that must be endured if they were to fulfill their wifely duty. The women of that age were afraid to let themselves go while engaging in sexual activity. They should have known that such sexual rigidity only encouraged their husbands to lust after other women who might make sex more fun. In one case study, Freud learned of a Victorian woman who, on her wedding night, drugged herself into unconsciousness, leaving a note for her husband which read, "Do to me what you must." God never intended sex to be viewed as a necessary evil, but rather as a glorious foretaste of heaven.

I am not suggesting that sex be devoid of reverence, thoughtfulness, kindness, and spiritual significance. On the contrary, I am suggesting that in sex we experience a whole gamut of godly emotions. Let's not forget that as laughter and joy belong to spirituality, so they belong in our sexual relationship as part of holiness. If sex in loving marital relationships is what God wills it to be, lust will lose its lure when contrasted with the ecstasy of love. The death of lust will come when the deadness of its consequences are compared with the vitality of the ordained culmination of love.

Those of you who are single are faced with an on-going struggle with sexual desires. I cannot pretend that living without sex is easy, and yet it is necessary if you are going to live according to a biblical morality. If you think I am saying, "You've got a painful and unresolved struggle on your hands for which we Christian preachers have no solution," you read me right. God does not diminish the sexual hungers of the single person, even though decent ways to gratify those hungers are not available. In short, it's a tough thing to be single and Christian at the same time. I can offer no effective consolation, except to quote from the Apostle Paul:

> Now concerning the unmarried, I have no command of the Lord, but I give my opinion as one who by the

Lord's mercy is trustworthy. . . . I want you to be free
from anxieties. The unmarried man is anxious about
the affairs of the Lord, how to please the Lord; but
the married man is anxious about worldly affairs, how
to please his wife, and his interests are divided. And
the unmarried woman or girl is anxious about the
affairs of the Lord, how to be holy in body and spirit;
but the married woman is anxious about worldly
affairs, how to please her husband (1 Cor. 7:25, 32-
34).

Lust is often an escape from boredom. Jesus came that our
joy might be full. He imparts His Holy Spirit to us, to fill us
so that we can live on a higher plane of fulfillment. Those of
us who work out our Christian commitment by serving soup
to street people must remember that the kingdom of God is
also a joyful banquet where there is singing and dancing
before the Lord. We must let the world know that the kingdom of God is celebration by demonstrating in our own lives
something of the joy we will know when His kingdom comes
on earth as it is in heaven. Even our sacrifices should be
expressions of joy, because joy is the fruit of the Spirit. Show
me a person who is singing songs, sharing laughter, bubbling
with the excitement of life, and I will show you a person who
is being delivered from the destructiveness of lust.

One problem with our age is that people have forgotten
how to experience passionate joy. They think that they must
go to Disneyland or have a VCR to be entertained. They
think that by getting *things* they will find fulfillment. All the
while a voice echoes down the corridors of time asking, "Why
do you spend your money for that which does not satisfy?"
The Christian life is a vitality in which the deadness of lust has
no place. In the words of Moses: "I call heaven and earth to
record this day against you, that I have set before you life and
death, blessing and cursing; therefore choose life that both
thou and thy seed may live" (Deut. 30:19, KJV).

CHAPTER THREE
ANGER

ANGER IS THE ONE deadly sin we all try to justify. We like to think that there are some circumstances in which anger is permissible. We even go so far as to make anger a defensible reaction in certain situations.

A man comes home unexpectedly and surprises his wife in bed with another man. In a fit of anger, he rushes to the bureau, pulls out a gun and shoots them both. In such circumstances, we sympathize with murder and call the killing of two people an excusable "crime of passion."

A fourteen-year-old girl is raped and traumatized for life. The assailant is tried and the judge prescribes a suspended sentence. As the rapist leaves the courthouse, he is accosted and stabbed to death by the angry mother of the violated child. We react to the news of this stabbing with a sense that justice has been done. "After all," we say, "who wouldn't want to do what she did?"

We all know that Jesus said, "Whosoever is angry with his brother without a cause shall be in danger of the judgment (Matt. 5:22, KJV). But how many of us know that the phrase, "without a cause," was added by the medieval scholar Erasmus? The *Revised Standard Version* and the *New International Version* of the Bible do not include the phrase. Erasmus was so desirous of justifying certain forms of anger that he was willing to change the words of Jesus in order to make his case. Jesus is harder on anger than Erasmus was, or, for that matter, than most of us might be. Jesus put anger in the same category as murder. If that seems harsh, just consider the consequences of anger in the lives of people and in the history of the world. Anger causes murder, provokes torture, leads to wars and a host of other cruel and diabolical crimes too ugly to mention. Anger stimulates spiteful actions that go far beyond retributive justice and usually result in the suffering of innocent people. It knows no limits as it leads to vengeance.

THE CAUSES OF ANGER

Anger is an emotional response to being unjustly humiliated. It involves a loss of self-esteem. The angry person feels outraged at what has been done to him/her and seeks to punish the perpetrator of the injustice. Vengeance, rather than justice, is sought. The angry person is carried away by the emotion and usually behaves in ways which can only be considered excessive.

A recent news story in the Philadelphia area told of a man who killed a driver who cut in front of him on the expressway. The murderer explained that traffic had slowed as it was funneled into a single lane. He claimed that he had waited in line for more than a quarter of an hour until he could begin to enter into the flow of traffic. Just as he was about to do so, another car passed him on the shoulder of the highway and cut in front of his automobile. As though that were not enough, the driver laughed and made an obscene gesture at him. It was too much for him to handle, and when traffic later stopped because of congestion, he removed a gun from his glove compartment, got out of his car, walked up to the side of the car of the man who had taunted him and shot him to death. The injustice of what had happened was bad enough, but being laughed at and taunted was more humiliation than he could tolerate.

When I was ten years old, my sister took me to a rodeo show at the Philadelphia Convention Hall. I loved the show, and to add to my joy, my sister bought me a felt cowboy hat from a vendor who assured this would-be bronco that the hats he was selling were straight from Texas.

The next day I proudly wore my hat so that all the kids in the neighborhood could admire it. Unexpectedly, an older boy who was almost twice my size grabbed my precious hat from my head and ran off with it. Hysterically I chased him, pleading with him to give me back what was mine. Suddenly, he stopped, turned on me, pushed me to the ground and held me down by sitting on my chest.

Then, for no reason except to be mean, he tore my hat in half. As I lay there helpless and in tears, I experienced an unforgettable surge of rage. The adrenalin that the anger generated gave me almost superhuman strength. I pushed my enemy off me, leaped on his back as he tried to escape, and began to scratch his face. He fell to the ground, and his head accidentally hit the curb. He was unconscious, but I did not care. With wild viciousness, I started to kick him, and if two men had not rushed to stop me, I might have kicked him to death. My anger came not simply from the injustice that had been dealt to me, but from humiliation and a loss of self-esteem.

ANGER IN THE HOME

The family provides the context for most expressions of anger. This is true for a variety of reasons, not the least of which is that in the home we feel less restraint from society. The family seems to be a separate world, distinct from the rest of our lives. We sense that we can express ourselves with our families without losing their affection and support. Most of us seem to think that it's okay to do things at home which we would never do outside.

Those most likely to exhibit outrageous behavior in the home are teenage children. I have been amazed to observe how young people treat their parents. They not only fail to honor them, but often humiliate them in unthinkable ways.

The problem is frequently most severe with the parent of the same sex as the teenager. Usually mothers (because they are often the most available) have incredibly painful times with their daughters. There are daughters who lash out at their mothers with derogatory names. They seem to feel that being a mother means enduring this kind of verbal abuse. Somehow they feel that have a right to emotional catharsis at the expense of their mothers. Seldom do they give any thought to the anguish which their mothers endure as they listen to the children's rantings. Fathers are more likely to be victims of such deplorable behavior from their sons. Young people seldom understand the anger that their parents experience when they are humiliated by those whom they love and for whom they have been willing to sacrifice so much of themselves.

Sometimes, after Christian young people have been off to a church camp or religious weekend retreat, they come home talking "the language of Zion" and, with pious platitudes, give testimonies of how their lives have been changed by God. However, none of this has any significance unless it changes the way they act at home. Those who have had genuine conversion experiences will give evidence of their new life in Christ by how they relate to their parents.

As I travel across America and talk to people, I realize how much pent-up anger there is in parents who have been humilated and dealt with unjustly by their children. Everywhere I go, I sense in parents a repressed rage at children who talk to them in denigrating ways. Such parents feel most helpless when their children are too old to be punished, and so the anger builds up more.

But children are not the only offenders in the home. Many children are victims of parental offenses and develop deep feelings of anger toward their parents because they feel humiliated by the unjust treatment. The child who is punished publicly often holds a grudge against the parent. Even when punishment is deserved, it should not be carried out where others can watch. To be paddled privately for some wrongdoing might be tolerable, but to be paddled in public seems an unforgivable humiliation.

It is important to remember that anger stems primarily from loss of self-esteem. The Bible gives clear instructions to parents: "Do not provoke your children to anger; but bring them up in the discipline and instruction of the Lord (Eph. 6:4). Surely this prohibits parents from punishing their children in such a way as to cause them unjustifiable embarrassment. Public punishment can have dire consequences, in that the accompanying loss of self-esteem may generate anger that leads to unimaginably evil deeds.

In a society in which divorce is increasingly common, children are often caught in the angry conflicts of their parents. The causes and process of divorce usually generate anger because divorce often holds a person up to public humiliation. To discover that one's spouse has "cheated" in a marriage is extremely painful; but when that adultery becomes public, the sense of disgrace is even more emotionally devastating. It is a horrible thing to have one's friends and relatives know that his/her spouse prefers another partner. The hurt is intense and the humiliation is often overwhelming. It is not surprising that in such circumstances a person can experience uncontrollable anger.

The divorce process itself is so structured that even those who seek to end a marriage amicably tend to develop deep feelings of anger toward each other. Divorce lawyers may resort to unfair tactics and try to depict the mates of their clients in the worst possible light. Frequently, to gain some advantage in a settlement, a lawyer will bring up ugly behavior from the past which will make the other party seem thoroughly perverted or evil. The humiliation endured in the courtroom can cause abiding anger to seethe in the consciousness of the partner who has been so exposed. Unfortunately, the children can end up as the victims of this anger, if their parents use them to get back at each other.

I know of one case in which a parent deliberately violated the visitation rights of his former wife. He refused to have the child ready to be picked up on days when she was entitled to have the child, knowing he could upset her by making her wait half an hour when she came to his house. His anger motivated his meanness and his meanness made his wife increasingly angry. The child who loved both of her parents was torn apart emotionally by their anger toward each other.

REACTIONS TO ANGER

I know a man whose motto is: "Don't get mad, get even." Anger stimulates a seemingly uncontrollable urge to strike back at the person who has humiliated you or unscrupulously wronged you. Anger generates fantasies of ways to make the offender suffer and repent. Anger stimulates a longing to see the evildoer writhe in psychological, if not physical, agony for the crimes committed.

Edgar Allen Poe's classic tale, "The Cask of Amontillado," tells the story of an Italian nobleman named Montresor who, with infinite patience, premeditated the murder of his friend Fortunato, whose treatment of him he interpreted as injurious and insulting. Montresor anticipated the prospect of revenge with great pleasure and with such control that Fortunato was unaware of his intent until he faced death. In Poe's story, as in the true incident which inspired it, the crime went undiscovered and unpunished. Vengeance was complete, but at what cost to the avenger?

In the somewhat violent high school subculture in which I spent my teenage years, there was a big tough guy who daily extorted money from younger students. It was not enough for him that he took money from boys who could never stand up to his bullying—but, at times, he would tell his victims to beg him to take their money. He got immense pleasure from forcing boys to do this in the presence of their girlfriends and then laughing at their humiliation.

One day at lunchtime, he picked on a boy whose brother was a 225-pound, six-feet five-inch center on the basketball team. Halfway through his extortion act, he felt a tap on his shoulder. He turned and was greeted by a solid punch to the stomach. In the face of the threat posed by his attacker, the tyrant became a sniveling coward begging not to be hit again. The crowd in the lunchroom roared with approval as the bully was told to get on his knees and beg for mercy. Not only did he do that, but he was forced to go to every other boy in the lunchroom and kiss his shoes. After that the bully transferred to another school. His public humiliation was more than he could bear. The rest of us were glad that he had gotten a taste of his own medicine. We felt he had had it coming.

When Rudolf Eichman, the Nazi war criminal, was captured and put on public display in a cage, we sensed something ugly in the treatment; but we could easily understand the desire of the victims of Auschwitz to seek vengeance on the architect of the Jewish holocaust.

Most examples of getting even are not so dramatic. I know of a secretary who was severely and, from her point of view, unjustly criticized for the way she did some of her work. Her coworkers all knew that the boss was displeased with her and she sensed that most of them agreed with his opinion. For several days she tried to go to work as though the criticism did not affect her, but it was to no avail. She was continually coming upon colleagues who seemed to suspend their conversation until after she was gone. Several times coworkers referred to the criticisms of the boss in their dealings with her. Eventually, she came to the point where she could no longer endure being put down, and decided to quit. Those in the office were not aware of the fact that essential papers and documents were filed according to a complex system that only she understood. When she left, the office systems were paralyzed because nobody could find anything. They tried to contact her, but she made herself unavailable. With great glee, she relished the confusion of those who had hurt her. Down deep inside she felt the satisfaction of having gotten even.

" 'Vengeance is mine; I will repay,' says the Lord" (Rom. 12:19), but few of us are willing to accept that arrangement. After a ten-year-old boy had been pushed into the mud by a nasty classmate, he was told that it was unnecessary to try to get even because God punishes evildoers. He responded, "Okay, I'll give God till Saturday."

For a variety of reasons, getting even is not a healthy response to anger. First of all, it cheapens and diminishes us. I had a friend who was a doctor in a Third World country ruled by an evil dictator. The ruler wanted to build a new clinic for my friend so that the sick in the village might have a decent place for medical care. My friend was so full of anger against the dictator that he refused to accept the offer. He told me that there was no way he was going to help that evil man look good in the eyes of the townspeople, after all the rotten things he had done. He gave a speech in the village market boldly declaring that his refusal to accept the gift from the nation's president was his way of "spitting in his face." My friend failed in his effort to get even. Instead his refusal generated feeling of disgust and disillusionment among the villagers. Their once-respected doctor they now saw as petty and mean, willing to deny them a much-needed medical facility just to satisfy his anger and pride. The attempt at vengeance cheapened my friend and diminished him in the eyes of those he wanted to serve.

One of my reasons for opposing capital punishment is that it diminishes the humanity of those who demand it. When we murder a murderer, we become something less than God intends us to be. Furthermore, vengeance seldom provides us with a sense that justice has been done.

Recently a man who had raped, robbed, and murdered a sixteen-year-old girl was put to death in the electric chair. The dead girl's father demanded and got the right to be present for the execution. When the ordeal was over, the father was interviewed by a reporter and simply said, "I wanted him to suffer more for what he did. Dying isn't enough!"

Our acts of vengeance are never enough. The death of a perverted man is not sufficient recompense for the death of a lovely young girl. There is seldom equity in the simple exchange of the life of the murderer for the life of the innocent. Vengeance leaves those who seek it with a sense of having been cheated. It brings a hollow victory. To those who cry, "An eye for an eye; a tooth for a tooth," one can offer the response that Gandhi once gave: "Following that philosophy will leave the world filled with blind, toothless people."

God specifically commanded Moses to instruct the people of Israel on the subject of vengeance: "You shall not hate your brother in your heart, but you shall reason with your neighbor, lest you bear sin because of him. You shall not take vengeance or bear any grudge against the sons of your own people, but you shall love your neighbor as yourself: I am the Lord" (Lev. 19:17-18).

There is increasing evidence that the vengeful themselves end up suffering for their desire to get even. Studies exploring the linkage between psychological and physiological conditions are discovering that obsession with vengeance may be a cause of such a diverse array of ailments as arthritis, asthma, and heart disease. The emotions that vengeful people experience often create a chemical imbalance in their bodies that can have dire consequences. I do not mean to suggest that these ailments are always traceable to vengeful emotions; but there is little question among some researchers that vengeful feelings are deleterious to health.

Some people who cannot get even handle their anger by suppressing it. This is the coping mechanism often used by religious people who try to pretend that they have forgotten all about the evildoers and are not going to let themselves be bothered by such people. We religious types often pretend that we are bigger than we really are, and we try to convince others that we have risen above becoming angry when we are publicly wronged. It maybe all right to convince others, but we should never deceive ourselves. Usually we *are* angered and we *do* want vengeance, but we pretend that things are otherwise. We suppress our anger and keep secret our ugly urge for revenge. In time we *think* we have forgotten all about what once angered us, but we should know better. We should know that nothing is ever *really* forgotten. Nothing is put out of our minds completely. We should know that what we suppress from our consciousness is only driven into the "underground" of our subconscious where it will haunt us without hindrance.

Psychologists tell us that the most likely consequence of suppressing anger is depression, and we know that there is a lot of depression around. When we suppress anger, we really unconsciously turn it in on ourselves and inner resentments eat away at our psyche, destroying our joy. When anger is turned inward via suppression, we end up hating ourselves and wanting ourselves to experience unhappiness and pain. Ironically, we get what we want and depression grows.

I am not suggesting that *all* depression results from suppressed anger, but I believe much of it does. This is especially true when the depression seems unfounded. When people tell me that they can find no reason for their depression, I ask them to search for suppressed anger.

As a boy, I was haunted by the phrase in 1 Corinthians that tells us that we may get sick or die if we celebrate Holy Communion without first confessing and getting rid of the sin in our hearts. "Let a man examine himself, and so eat of the bread and drink of the cup. For any one who eats and drinks without discerning the body eats and drinks judgment upon himself. That is why many of you are weak and ill, and some have died (1 Cor. 11:28-30).

Depth psychology concurs with the awesome truths of the Scriptures. How much depression is caused and how many suicides result when people come to Christ without having dealt with emotions that are too deep to put into words?

However, we must not be overawed by modern psychology, nor be too ready to accept the scientific prescriptions of its would-be healers of troubled souls. Psychiatrists and psychologists are often wrong. Sometimes their advice is poor. This is certainly true of much of what they say about handling anger. Often the "professionals" suggest that we get rid of our anger by expressing it. They advise us to experience the catharsis that comes from "working out" our anger and frustration. The angry child is given a teddy bear and told to punch it as though it were the parent who has made the child angry. The employee is told to play golf and hit the ball as though it were the boss. The wife is told to tell her husband off and not keep her emotions bottled up inside.

Certainly it is better to punch a teddy bear than a mother, hit a golf ball than a boss, and to scream at one's husband than to hate one's self; but there are dangers in expressing anger.

Expressing an emotion often causes us to feel the emotion even more intensely. Those who do loving acts usually feel love all the more. Those who do kind things usually end up feeling kind. And those who express anger usually end up feeling more angry. It may be healthier to express anger than to suppress it, but expressing anger usually intensifies it.

George Herbert Mead, one of America's foremost sociologists, discovered that what we say and do influences how we feel, as much as how we feel influences what we do. Feelings and actions reinforce each other. There is, according to Mead, interaction between them. We all should know this from experience. Who has not told someone off in a fit of anger, only to find that the expression of anger caused him or her to tremble with even greater rage when all was said and done?

What Mead pronounced in theory, and most of us have learned from experience, was profoundly stated a long time ago by James:

> For we all make mistakes, and if any one makes no mistakes in what he says he is a perfect man, able to

bridle the whole body also. If we put bits into the mouths of horses that they may obey us, we guide their whole bodies. Look at the ships also; though they are so great and are driven by strong winds, they are guided by a very small rudder wherever the will of the pilot directs. So the tongue is a little member and boasts of great things. How great a forest is set ablaze by a small fire! (James 3:2-5)

James wants us to recognize that what we say in anger can determine our destiny. There are consequences to what we say and do in the expression of anger, and we should weigh these consequences before we take the simplistic advice of those psychotherapists who tell us to do so for our health.

I can think of no more evil way to handle anger than to displace it—in other words, to take out our anger on the innocent. The newspapers these days report regularly on wife-abuse. In case after case, it becomes apparent that the victims of these beatings suffer because of displaced anger.

Men who have been humiliated at work, whose anger stems from their own limitations, and who hate themselves because they have failed to live up to expectations, express their pent-up aggression on those close to them. Usually these innocent and defenseless victims are their wives. And for every story that makes the papers, there are hosts of unreported cases. Angry men, who are unable to strike out at those they believe have wronged them, are dangerous to be around.

Wives are not the only victims of such displaced anger. Sometimes it is taken out on the elderly who are in no position to defend themselves. Often the victims of displaced anger are children, as hospital records clearly indicate. And surprisingly, there seems to be increasing incidence of husband-abuse. Even if wives do not hit their husbands, many of them find others ways of taking their anger out on them. Wives displace their pent-up anger by lashing out at their husbands verbally.

I knew a woman who always seemed to be scolding her husband and calling him denigrating names. I was amazed as I watched her afflict him with a seemingly endless flow of verbal barbs. One day when I was with him, I asked why he put up with painful treatment. He responded by telling me that several years before their son had died of cancer and that, as a result of that tragedy, his wife was angry with God. He went on to say, "She can't take out her anger on God, so I guess she has to take it out on me instead." He seemed to understand very well why his wife treated him so cruelly.

OVERCOMING ANGER

There are constructive and healthy ways of handling anger. Perhaps the following prescriptions will provide some helpful guidance in establishing a Christian approach to overcoming this deadly emotional condition.

First of all, when anger overtakes us, we should take time to reflect. Specifically, we should reflect on the grace which God has shown to us when we have done things that would justify His anger toward us. In one of His parables, Jesus encourages us to take this route of reflection.

> Therefore the kingdom of heaven may be compared to a king who wished to settle accounts with his servants. When he began the reckoning, one was brought to him who owed him ten thousand talents; and as he could not pay, his lord ordered him to be sold, with his wife and children and all that he had, and payment to be made. So the servant fell on his knees, imploring him, "Lord, have patience with me, and I will pay you everything." And out of pity for him the lord of that servant released him and forgave him the debt. But that same servant, as he went out, came upon one of his fellow servants who owed him a hundred denarii; and seizing him by the throat he said, "Pay what

you owe." So his fellow servant fell down and besought him, "Have patience with me, and I will pay
you." He refused and went and put him in prison till
he should pay the debt. When his fellow servants saw
what had taken place, they were greatly distressed, and
they went and reported to their lord all that had taken
place. Then his lord summoned him and said to him,
"You wicked servant! I forgave you all that debt because you besought me; and should not you have had
mercy on your fellow servant, as I had mercy on you?"
(Matt. 18:23-33)

When we think we have a right to be angry, Jesus reminds
us that God, who has every right to be angry with us, is
willing to remove our wrongs from the record. It is petty of
us to make others pay for their wrongdoing when the Heavenly Father has forgiven and forgotten our offenses.

God does not vent His wrath toward us even though we
deserve it. Instead He handles His wrath by having it borne
by His Son. The Scriptures teach us that the obedience of
Jesus manifested in His willingness to obey His Father's will
even to death on the cross served to allay God's anger toward
us. Jesus represented us in His obedient submission to the
Father's will, and because of that, God's anger toward us is no
more. That is the meaning behind Paul's words:

"Since all have sinned and fall short of the glory of
God, they are justified by His grace as a gift, through
the redemption which is in Christ Jesus, whom God
put forward as an expiation by His blood, to be
received by faith. This was to show God's righteousness, because in His divine forbearance He had passed
over former sins" (Rom. 3:23-25).

An expiation is a gift that overcomes the wrath of someone
who is offended. No other gift offered up on behalf of those

of us who should have incurred the just anger of God can match what Jesus gave, as He offered Himself up for us all. In light of the love which took Jesus to the cross, there is little justification for our bearing grudges toward those who have angered us.

A friend of mine tells the story of a mountaineer from West Virginia who fell in love with the beautiful daughter of the town preacher. The gruff and tough man one evening looked deeply into the eyes of the preacher's daughter and said, "I love you." It took more courage for him to say those simple words than he had ever had to muster for anything else he had ever done. Minutes passed in silence and then the preacher's daughter said, "I love you too."

The tough mountaineer said nothing except, "Good night." Then he went home, got ready for bed and prayed, "God, I ain't got nothin' against nobody."

When a person is loved, there seems to be little room for anger in his life. Love drives anger out of his mind and heart, for life is too wonderful to allow anger to creep in and spoil it.

If each of us would reflect on the good news that God loves us, and would be open to His love, we could be transformed into people who "ain't got nothin' against nobody." The first step to overcoming anger is to reflect on what Jesus has done for us and how much He loves us.

Secondly, we must learn that the Bible teaches us that there is justice in God's economy. There is no need for us to seek revenge for wrongs done against us. There is a God who sets things right. Nobody gets away with sin forever.

Even if we did not have the Bible's revelation about our afterlife, we would know it existed—cosmic justice demands it. There must be a place and time, beyond space and time as we know them, where the unrepentant who have hurt people will be made to pay for what they have done. The Bible assures us that there is such a place. Mean people do not get away with their meanness. Corrupt people do not get away with their evil. Oppressors do not get away with what they do to the weak and helpless. Tyrants and petty thieves pay for what they do. In the words of Friedrich Van Logauz:

> Though the mills of God grind slowly, yet they grind exceeding small;
> Though with patience He stands waiting, with exactness grinds He all.

To those who are oppressed, James writes, "Be patient, therefore, brethren, until the coming of the Lord. Behold, the farmer waits for the precious fruit of the earth, being patient over it until it receives the early and the late rain. You also be patient. Establish your hearts, for the coming of the Lord is at hand" (James 5:7-9).

There is no need for us to seethe in anger and seek revenge; in the end, justice will come from God. However, the final Christian resolution to anger comes from deciding to imitate the style of Jesus and doing good for those who have made us angry. What we do influences how we feel, and that means that our feelings can be changed by what we decide to do. In short, there are things we can do to overcome anger. There are ways that anger can be dealt with creatively and biblically. However, when all those ways are analyzed, they can be summed up in one statement: Do good to those who hurt you, or despitefully use you, or do all manner of evil against you.

Victor Frankl, the famous psychoanalyst, was imprisoned in one of Hitler's concentration camps. He was stripped of all his dignity, abused, and tortured. He was starved and forced into slave labor. There were many in the concentration camp who did not survive, not because they were put into gas chambers, but because they found that survival was intolerable. They were the ones who were eaten up with rage against their oppressors. The humiliation meted out to them by their Nazi dominators could not be resisted, and the overwhelming injustice was too much for them to endure. Therefore, they chose to die. Nobody overtly killed them; they gave up living.

Victor Frankl had another answer which was as old as the Sermon on the Mount. He decided to do good for those who wronged him. His decision was in line with what Jesus asked His followers to do:

> And if any one would sue you and take your coat, let him have your cloak as well; and if any one forces you to go one mile, go with him two miles. Give to him who begs from you, and do not refuse him who would borrow from you.
>
> You have heard it said, "You shall love your neighbor and hate your enemy." But I say to you, "Love your enemies and pray for those who persecute you" (Matt. 5:40-44).

When his captors asked him to scrub latrines with a toothbrush, he would do it twice. He did it once because he had to and the second time because he willed to. He turned the situation in which he was being humiliated into one in which he willingly served others. By redefining the situation in a positive way, he learned that he could overcome his hatred and anger toward his oppressors.

It is unlikely that we will be placed in circumstances as evil as those experienced by Victor Frankl, but his way of dealing with rage is applicable in all situations. Do for those who make you angry more than they ask of you. Do good for them and serve them.

In my mid-twenties, I served as the pastor of a church. Looking back on those years, I realize that my inexperience and lack of maturity sometimes led me to do things that unnecessarily offended some of my parishioners. On the other hand, there were some people in that church who were not kind to me. One particular woman seemed determined to have me ousted from my job. She did everything she could to make my life miserable. I could count on some weekly act of meanness from her. For quite a while, I felt myself growing increasingly angry with her. What she was doing to me seemed so unfair and cruel. Her treatment of me seemed so un-Christian. Almost everyone to whom I told my story agreed that I was justified in my feelings toward her, that the ways in which she tried to humiliate me in the eyes of the congregation were evil. Only my wife did not defend my attitude.

My wife is one of those rare people who always has compassion for wrongdoers, because she is convinced that their actions are expressions of their own unhappiness. Peggy persuaded me to be nice to my tormentor and to seek ways to make her feel good. I did my best. I took her to special denominational meetings, gave her public recognition for any positive thing she did for the church, and sent her postcards when I was on trips. I'm not sure how much all of these kindnesses changed her feelings about me, but I do know that I was changed by them. Little by little, I realized that the more I did for that lady, the more I liked her. I learned what Jesus taught—the more I serve a person with whom I justifiably could be angry, the less angry I feel.

I know of a woman whose husband had been unfaithful to her. What made the matter worse was that the sexual affair had been carried on with her best friend. My friend had been betrayed by the two people in the world she trusted most. The whole sordid affair had taken place right under her nose, but she loved both her husband and her friend so much that she had failed to notice what was happening. It wasn't until her friend's husband followed the adulterous couple to a motel, and then told her the story, that she realized how she had been deceived. At first, she was filled with rage and let her repentant husband and friend experience something of the fury she felt. Later she went for counseling and asked her Christian psychologist what she should do. He wisely advised her to overcome evil with good.

Following that advice, my friend went out of her way to be

kind to those who had betrayed her. She went so far as to have several talks with her friend's husband and was able to persuade him to give his marriage a second chance. As she worked for the good of her unfaithful friend, her bitterness subsided and her love for her friend was rekindled. She found it harder to overcome her bitterness toward her husband, but eventually, by following the same formula, she was able to conquer her anger, and work with her husband toward building mutual trust and love.

My last illustration of how this method of handling anger can work in the desperate situations of life comes from the story of one of the ugliest murders in the history of the City of Philadelphia. In April of 1958, a twenty-six-year-old Korean graduate student who was studying political science at the University of Pennsylvania went out to mail a letter. Before he could get back to his apartment, he was accosted by a gang of violent teenagers looking for money to go to a dance. They robbed and killed him. This young man had been a model son and an exemplary Christian. He had graduated from Eastern College where I teach.

Those who committed the crime were the most contemptible of people. They seemed to sneer at the authorities who accused them, and they appeared arrogant as they were brought to trial. The widowed mother of their victim had every right to be filled with anger against these haughty criminals, but she was not. The members of her church in Korea took up an offering to provide funds for her to come to the United States so that she could help those who had committed the crime that had hurt her so deeply.

When the young hoods who murdered her son were tried and found guilty, she got down on her knees before the judge to plead that their lives be spared. What she did brought the first positive response from the murderers. They began to weep and express their sorrow. Tears came to the eyes of the policemen who held the young criminals in chains. And Philadelphia witnessed something of the extent to which the love of God can be lived out in a believer. I am not sure what went on in the mind and heart of that dear Christian woman, but I am almost certain that what she did for those who had killed her son made it impossible for her to be angry with them.

Anger is self-defeating, it is self-destructive, and it is contrary to the will of God. Anger motivates us to do things which are inconsistent with Christian values. "The anger of man does not work the righteousness of God" (James 1:20).

CHAPTER FOUR

PRIDE

SAVANAROLA, the great Florentine preacher of the fifteenth century, one day saw an elderly woman worshiping at the statue of the Virgin Mary which stood in his city's great cathedral. On the following day, he noticed the same woman again on her knees before the Blessed Mother. With great interest, Savonarola observed that day after day, she came and did homage before the statue.

"Look how she reverences the Virgin Mother," Savanarola whispered to one of his fellow priests.

"Don't be deceived by what you see," the priest responded. "Many years ago an artist was commissioned to create a statue for the cathedral. As he sought a young woman to pose as the model for his sculpture, he found one who seemed to be the perfect subject. She was young, serenely lovely, and had a mystical quality in her face. The image of that young woman inspired his statue of Mary. The woman who now worships the statue is the same one who served as its model years ago. Shortly after the statue was put in place, she began to visit it and has continued to worship there religiously ever since."

Pride is arrogant self-worship. It is the sin of exalting oneself and placing one's own interests above the interests of others. Pride craves admiration and even adoration, and will not share the limelight. Pride deludes its victims into believing that they have no peers and drives them to try to destroy anyone who takes recognition away from them. The proud are in love with themselves and seek to call attention to their admirable qualities.

Pride is a primary barrier to salvation. God has provided for our deliverance from sin through the death of His Son. We are saved by putting our faith in Christ and believing that His death atoned for our sin. Salvation is not something that we earn, but comes as a gift from a gracious God. "For by grace are ye saved through faith; and that not of yourselves; it is the gift of God" (Eph. 2:8).

Pride makes it difficult for many of us to accept this gift. We have a tendency to want to be saved because we are somehow worthy of God's blessings. Our pride drives us to want to earn our salvation by doing enough good deeds so that the Heavenly Father will owe us eternal life. But this is not the plan God has devised. Rather, He requires us to humble ourselves, acknowledge our inability to live righteous lives, repent of our sins, and depend only on His grace.

We prideful people have trouble with this plan because it renders our own good deeds and personal achievements worthless. "Not by works of righteousness which we have done, but according to His mercy He saved us, by the washing of regeneration, and renewing of the Holy Ghost" (Titus 3:5, KJV). As spiritually impoverished sinners, our only hope for salvation lies in God's gift, yet pride leads us to try to prove our worth to God. God despises our pride and calls us to trust only in Jesus who was willing to humble Himself and become the ultimate servant of humanity.

Even among evangelical Christians who say that they are saved by grace, I find blatant expressions of pride. I am amazed to discover how many of those who claim to be in Christ still believe that their own righteousness will earn them credit with God. They do not claim that their good works will gain them access *to* heaven, just status *in* heaven. They are convinced that by serving Jesus here on earth, they can improve the position they will occupy when they get to heaven. But whenever Christian service is rendered with hope of reward, it is not really Christian at all. That any of us should seek superiority over the rest of us is anti-Christian and a contradiction of the Gospel. That anyone should even think about being better off than others in heaven is an expression of a prideful disposition that is unworthy of a follower of Jesus. Nevertheless, I have heard Christians complain about the injustice of deathbed converts receiving the same rewards in heaven as longtime Christians.

It was against this kind of prideful thinking that Jesus was speaking in the Parable of the Vineyard. At harvest, a man bargained with laborers to work in his vineyard for a fixed daily wage. As the day passed, he hired others to work for fewer hours at the same daily wage. When those who had begun to work in the morning complained about this arrangement, the man responded: "Is it not lawful for me to do what I will with mine own? Is thine eye evil, because I am good? So the last shall be first, and the first shall be last: for many be called, but few chosen (Matt. 20:15-16).

PRIDE INFECTS THE SPIRIT

Pride infects Christians in a variety of ways that can spoil their commitment to Christ. I have known some missionaries to be caught up in their own nobility as they minister in the name of Christ. Like the Pharisees in the days of our Lord, some of them want people to acknowledge their sacrificial lifestyle and tell them how wonderful they are.

I find that the easiest way to escape from the pitfall of pride while serving others in the name of Christ is to remember His words:

> Then shall the King say unto them on His right hand, "Come, ye blessed of My Father, inherit the kingdom prepared for you from the foundation of the world.
> "For I was an hungered, and ye gave Me meat; I was thirsty, and ye gave Me drink; I was a stranger,

and ye took Me in; Naked, and ye clothed Me; I was
sick, and ye visited Me; I was in prison, and ye came
unto Me."

Then shall the righteous answer Him, saying,
"Lord, when saw we Thee an hungered, and fed Thee?
or thirsty and gave Thee drink? When saw we Thee a
stranger, and took Thee in? or naked, and clothed
Thee? Or when saw we Thee sick, or in prison, and
came unto Thee?"

And the King shall answer and say unto them,
"Verily I say unto you, Inasmuch as ye have done it
unto one of the least of these My brethren, ye have
done it unto Me" (Matt. 25:34-40).

If I can serve others as if I were serving Jesus, I am delivered
from any feelings of nobility in what I do. It is one thing to
lift some drunk out of the gutter, take him home, shower him
and put him into my bed. In such a case I might view myself
as a wonderful person who did something worthy of praise.
On the other hand, if when I look into the eyes of that drunk,
I think of ministering to Jesus Himself, I am only left inquir-
ing of myself, "Am I worthy?"

To recognize the image of our God in even the most
socially despised of creatures is to become a humble servant of
these people.

Pride mars so many ministries. As a young pastor, I caught
myself time and time again going into the pulpit more concerned about what kind of image I was projecting to my
congregation than about how much glory I would bring to
God. Even in the midst of Christian service, I found myself
seduced into seeking personal recognition rather than the
spiritual well-being of those who had come to hear the Gospel. I constantly needed to repent of the sin of pride.

One of the most disturbing practices among American
pastors is the promotion of unnecessary church building programs. Because we can glorify God through art forms, there is

a place for magnificent architecture. However, from one end of this country to the other, there are tens of thousands of church buildings with low aesthetic value, many of which do little more than provide gratification for the egos of the pastors and committees who plan them. Someone has sarcastically suggested that many American clergy suffer from an "edifice complex." A number of the church buildings being constructed are unnecessary, because their congregations will underuse them. Some of these groups could rent a local school or theater at a fraction of the cost of a new building, or facilities could be shared by two or three congregations.

There are ways for churches to have places for worship and Christian education without entailing the exorbitant cost of new buildings. Nevertheless, the construction will go on because the pride of pastors and church leaders demands it. No matter that the money going into bricks and mortar is desperately needed to feed a half billion hungry people. No matter that the financial resources given for buildings that glorify pastors could be used to save some of the 40,000 children in our world who starve to death each day. No matter that the funds spent on structures that will be fully used for only a few hours a week are essential to finance the propagation of the Gospel to the billion people who have not heard the story of God's salvation. Pride, not need, often determines how money given to churches will be spent. Paul tells us: "Do nothing from selfishness or conceit but in humility count others better than yourselves" (Phil. 2:3). Unfortunately, those members of the clergy who are obsessed with buildings have failed to get this message.

When I was in seminary, I had to take a course in homiletics under Professor Albert G. Williams. This dear saint of God required each of us to preach a sermon that he and the members of the class would evaluate. I vividly remember delivering my homily. It was well-constructed with three points which I deemed to be profound and biblically sound. The body of the sermon was laced with illustrations and witticisms. I delivered the sermon with practiced gestures and made sure to employ the techniques of proper eye contact with my listeners. In short, I knew I was good.

Following the class, I was handed a bundle of papers containing the evaluations of my fellow students. They offered praise for my sermon and assured me that I would really go places after graduation. The last evaluation in the pile was from Professor Williams. He did not comment on the content of my message or on its delivery. His one sentence was concise and cutting: "Tony, you can't convince people that you're wonderful and that Jesus is wonderful in the same sermon." I have never forgotten that simple line. Remembering it just before I preach acts as a safeguard against using my sermon as a prideful play for recognition.

A friend of mine visited the church of one of the prominent preachers on the American scene. When the worship service was over and the crowd dispersing, he stood talking with an elderly church woman. Suddenly, their conversation was disrupted by the shout of the pastor's young son who had run up into the pulpit, seized the microphone, and shouted, "Look everybody, I'm in the pulpit!" With disgust the elderly woman said, "His father preaches that every Sunday." What a telling commentary! It would be well for any of us who occupy the sacred desk to remember that those gathered before us are waiting to see Jesus.

Pride keeps us from knowing the truth about ourselves. Those who are infected with pride can never become spiritual because they are unable to face up to those facets of their lives which are evil and need repentance. When I was teaching at the University of Pennsylvania, I had a Jewish colleague who was greatly taken with himself. I was surprised when I met him at school on the high Jewish holiday, Yom Kippur. The Day of Atonement is observed by devout Jews throughout the world and I assumed that my colleague would fulfill this religious obligation. When I said, "I thought you would be in the synagogue, observing Yom Kippur," he replied, "I have done nothing for which I must atone." A friend who was with me whispered in my ear, "I think the guy is serious!"

While most of would not make such blatantly prideful statements, we are often not much different from my colleague! How often we justify ourselves when we are caught in an error or a sin. I have a friend who apologizes in such a way as to make himself seem to be innocent. On one occasion after deliberately hurting someone with a cutting remark, he apologized by saying, "I'm sorry. I guess I'm too honest for my own good." His pride enabled him to see what he did as a consequence of his virtue rather than an expression of his meanness. On another occasion he marched out of an important conference, leaving the rest of us devastated by his abrupt treatment. Later he apologized by saying, "Please forgive me, but you people were saying intolerable things about me, and I couldn't just sit there and listen to you when I thought you were totally unfair." Once again his nasty behavior was explained away as evidence of his virtue and our shortcomings. He could never recognize any faults in himself.

Jesus had harsh judgments for the Pharisees for exactly the same reason. These godly people endeavored to live righteously in accord with biblical principles. They prided themselves on being better than other people, and that was their sin. Jesus commented graphically on this attitude:

> Two men went up into the temple to pray; the one a Pharisee, and the other a publican.
>
> The Pharisee stood and prayed thus with himself, "God, I thank Thee, that I am not as other men are, extortioners, unjust, adulterers or even as this publican. I fast twice in the week, I give tithes of all that I possess."
>
> And the publican, standing afar off, would not lift up so much as his eyes unto heaven, but smote upon his breast, saying, "God, be merciful to me a sinner" (Luke 18:10-13).

Jesus wanted the Pharisees to know that salvation was available only to those who could recognize their spiritual inadequacies. Inasmuch as they were unable to acknowledge their own sinfulness, there was no help for them.

Ironically there is another kind of spiritual pride that is a reaction to Pharisaism. It is manifested in those who are proud that they can publicly acknowledge their evil ways. In some evangelistic services, testimonies are given by celebrities who delight the crowds with stories of their lurid pasts. Those of us who have never been on drugs or indulged in sexual promiscuity feel like second-class Christians by the time they finish telling us about all the things from which the Lord has delivered them. They seem to be making the point that they are more spiritual than the rest of us because the Lord has done more for them. It is a temptation to fabricate stories about the past, painting pictures of escapades which never took place, simply because we know how impressed some people will be with a dramatic testimony.

When I was pastor of a small Baptist church, a woman brought her ten-year-old daughter to me and told me that it was time for her to be baptized. It was the custom at this church that all candidates for baptism were required to give a testimony of their Christian experience at midweek prayer meeting prior to the baptism. When her turn came, this ten-year-old girl rose and piously started her testimony with the words, "For years I wandered deep in sin, fulfilling all the lusts of the flesh." The poor child had heard adults win admiration from the church people by telling of former perverse behavior. Since she lacked a lurid past, she was prepared to invent one.

I was told of a man who came home drunk after a night of carousing in a number of neighborhood bars. His wife helped him up to the bedroom, helped him to undress and tucked him into bed. Then she kneeled at his bedside and whispered, "John, do you want me to pray for you?" He nodded a yes and she began to pray, "Dear Lord, I pray for my husband who lies here drunk. . . . " Before she could finish, he said gruffly, "Don't tell Him I'm drunk; tell Him I'm sick." There is a perverse humor to this story and yet it is the story of all of us who, in our pride, cannot truthfully acknowledge our deplorable condition. Scripture is very clear: "If we confess our sins, He is faithful and just and will forgive our sins and cleanse us from all unrightousness" (1 John 1:9).

PRIDE RUINS RELATIONSHIPS
Pride keeps us not only from God, but from each other. In order to elicit the admiration of others we deceive one another. Our pride hinders us from being open and honest. We would rather have people admire the selves we pretend to be than to love the selves we really are. In Arthur Miller's *Death of a Salesman,* the tragic Willy Loman is so anxious to convey the impression that he is a successful businessman who knows how to handle people, that he conceals his frightened, lonely self from his closest friends and even from his wife. He becomes a solitary man who lives out his days in desperate isolation. His pride keeps him from the kind of self-revelation essential for meaningful relationships.

Sociologist Erving Goffman contends that society is nothing more than a complex system of con jobs in which we try to convince each other that we are something we are not. He says that doctors try to inspire awe in their patients by pretending to be able to diagnose what they really do not understand; that lawyers pretend to know exactly what the law allows when in reality they are very limited; and that teachers present themselves to their students as possessing more knowledge than they really possess. Goffman claims that pride makes con artists of us all.

It seems to me that one of the most important dimensions of salvation through Christ is deliverance from the dishonesty that stems from pride. When you come to an awareness of how important you are to Jesus, you see your boasting as hollow and meaningless. If you view yourself as so special to God that He would have sent His Son to die just for you, you find that playing games to establish a sense of importance becomes unnecessary.

When you recognize that the righteousness of Christ has been ascribed to you, you know that any attempt to add to your image through righteousness of your own is ridiculous. When you are in Christ, you do not need the praise of others to maintain your identity.

Once we become aware of who we are with God, we can afford to be open and honest with others because we no longer fear their rejection. And once we can dare to be open and honest about ourselves with others, we are able to enter into deep relationships with them. False pride leads us to deceive one another. Knowing ourselves in Jesus delivers us from foolish pride and gives us the grace to make ourselves transparent to each other.

Many people who consider themselves Christians remain at odds with each other because their pride will not allow them to make the confessions necessary for reconciliation. There is the father who in an angry tirade orders his son out of the house, and then anguishes over what he has done. But pride prevents him from going to his son to say that he is sorry. There is the deacon who verbally attacks his pastor at a church business meeting, and stomps out of the church in a huff. He misses the fellowship of his former church friends, but will not confess his sin because he is afraid of losing face. Pride so often acts as a barrier to reconciliation, but there is a remedy for this kind of alienation in the example of Christ. He did not wait for us to come to Him confessing our sin and begging forgiveness. The Bible tells us that while we were still in our sinful state, Jesus took our sin upon Himself. What He did for us, we should be willing to do for others.

What this means in practical terms is that when someone wrongs you, you should not make that person's repentance the basis upon which reconciliation can begin. Rather, you should recognize that his pride will probably keep him from taking that important step. Therefore, you should go to him, assume the guilt for what has happened, and take the sin upon yourself. Pray yourself to the point where you can take the blame for what has happened. Remember that is exactly what Jesus did for you on the cross.

There is a strong likelihood that once you have taken this difficult step and the offending party no longer finds self-justification necessary, there *will* be repentance. People are far more willing to repent when they realize that they will not be condemned if they do. At that point they are free to look at themselves with honesty and recognize what *they* did that was sinful. It is probable that when you go to the person who has hurt you, and acknowledge that you are to blame for what has happened, the offending party will say, "I'm responsible too," and will confess his failures. We can help people to overcome their prideful self-righteousness by rendering such an attitude unnecessary.

PRIDE DESTROYS THOSE WE LOVE

The pride of parents can lead to the destruction of children. People who are out to prove that they are better than others often use their children to achieve this end. We will never know how many children have had their lives made miserable by being pushed to achievements which make their parents look good. Children who are driven to psychological exhaustion for academic achievement often know that their labor is primarily to enhance the status of their parents. Behind the claims that the parents expect the children to do well, because success in school will increase their options, is the ugly reality that the achievements of the children visibly demonstrate the superiority of the parents.

Sports are ruined for many teenagers. There is not much fun on most varsity teams because there is a deadly seriousness about the games being played. From Little League through interscholastic sports, the omnipresent parents are pushing their children in order to gratify their own ego needs.

Another expression of the prideful exploitation of children can be witnessed in the beauty contests for teenage girls and even for children. Recently, I saw a television special about little girls competing for such dubious titles as Miss Junior Miss. With stark amazement, I watched interviews with parents who admitted that they pushed their daughters through arduous routines so that they might become winners. It took very little analysis to discover that the parents were nurturing a desire to achieve success through their children.

As I watched those girls mastering the techniques of women who have become the sex objects of our society, I wondered how long it would be before many of them would be destroyed by the parents' desires for recognition.

Even young marriages can be manipulated to serve the interests of parents. We all know of parents who reject the prospective mates their children have chosen because they think these potential sons or daughters-in-law are beneath them. Since the status of women is significantly influenced by the men they marry, some parents try to prevent marriages which will diminish a daughter's position in society. Such parents are sometimes more concerned what others will think of the mate their daughter selects than about whether she will be happy. Happiness is often a casualty of pride.

Other forms of exploitation of children are evident in Christian circles. I wonder how many people have been pushed into church vocations because of the pride of parents. When I taught in seminary, I was well aware of the fact that many of my students were studying for the ministry, not because God had called them, but because being ministers of the Gospel would serve the ego needs of their parents.

As a preacher, I would like to be able to say that my son or my daughter is in the ministry. But why? Is it because I believe that they will find spiritual fulfillment in such positions and actualize their God-given potential? Is it because I believe God has ordained them to such service? Or is it because my pride drives me to want to brag about the fact that my children want to follow in my footsteps?

In some cases it is pride rather than love that makes parents want their children to have a salvation experience. They want to be able to say pompously, "Train up a child in the way he should go, and when he is old, he will not depart from it" (Prov. 22:6). Pride can pervert the motivation of even the noblest objectives.

Perhaps the most ugly expression of pride that destroys children is seen in incest. Recent studies reveal that in most situations where fathers have been exploiting their daughters sexually, the mothers are well aware of what is happening. However, these mothers usually allow the sexual molestations to continue and say little or nothing, because they are afraid of the shame of prosecution. These mothers are willing to sacrifice the psychological and physical well-being of their daughters rather than to endure the humiliation of exposing their husbands for what they really are. They may urge their daughters to say nothing about what is going on, or even worse, may pretend that they do not believe the stories their daughters tell them. The preservation of pride can lead to unspeakably cruel treatment of children whom parents profess to love.

PRIDE CAN DESTROY A NATION

"Pride goeth before destruction, and a haughty spirit before a fall" (Prov. 16:18). That warning not only applies to personal relationships but is particularly applicable to what goes on at the societal level. I am convinced that the United States has its greatest enemy in itself. The pride of America, more than any other single factor, threatens our existence as a nation.

I first became aware of the extremes to which national pride could carry us during the Vietnam War. I will always remember the shocking words of President Nixon: "I will not be the first President of the United States to lose a war."

There was no talk of the rightness of the war or the concerns of justice. There was no discussion of what this war was costing America. All that seemed to matter was that the pride of the president be kept intact. President Nixon may have had noble motives for pursuing a military struggle that cost the lives of over 40,000 American soldiers and left half a million of them scarred for life. I want to believe that there was more than national pride and the face-saving of an American president at stake in that painful conflict. However, there is no doubt that because our leaders found the humiliation of defeat too much to endure, the Vietnam War continued long after it became evident that it could not be won. There is a gigantic price to be paid for pride.

As we find ourselves caught up in an incredible arms race with the Soviet Union, I am beginning to wonder whether it is national defense or national pride that drives us to build bigger and more devastating bombs. I wonder whether it is our fear of being destroyed by the Russians or our compulsion to be the number-one nation in the world that is responsible for our willingness to spend ourselves into national bankruptcy in order to feed our military machine. The Prophet Isaiah once offered this warning to the Children of Israel: "Woe to them that go down to Egypt for help; and stay on horses, and trust in chariots, because they are many; and in horsemen, because they are very strong; but they look not unto the Holy One of Israel, neither seek the Lord!" (Isa. 31:1)

It would be well for us to heed that warning today. Our pride will lead us to trust in our own strength for our salvation. We would be wise to humble ourselves as a nation, repent and trust in the Lord.

DEVELOP HEALTHY HUMILITY

A common mistake among evangelical Christians is to confuse humility with humiliation and to think that pride can be overcome through self-contempt. Humility enhances our humanity and makes us more like Christ, whereas humiliation diminishes our humanity and tempts us to forget that we are made in the image of God.

John Perkins, the founder of Voice of Calvary, gives us one of the most moving illustrations of the destructiveness of humiliation in a touching story from his youth.

I was about eleven years old when I got a powerful lesson in economics. It was a lesson which helped me see why poor families like mine stayed poor while the rich got richer.

I stood on a farmer's back porch, waiting for him to come back with the money. I was bone tired, that good kind of tired that comes after a hard day's work. The kind of tired a boy earns from doing a man's worth of hauling on a hot, humid summer day in Mississippi.

But if my body was remembering the day's work, my mind was flying ahead to what I could do with the dollar or dollar and a half that would soon be in my pocket. Would I buy a shiny new pocket knife? That would really wow the guys back home. Or what about a wallet?

Not that I really needed these things, you see. But I *was* a few miles away from home. For kids in our town that was big stuff. Vacations were always an occasion for bragging—so much that the kids who did not go on vacations had to invent them.

So that's how this thing got started, this custom of buying something while you're gone to prove where you've been. What I bought wasn't all that important. What was important was what it would prove.

The farmer came through the kitchen onto the back porch. I held out my hand expectantly. Into it fell—I could hardly believe it—just two coins! A dime and a buffalo nickel! I stared into my hand. If that farmer would have knocked the wind out of me, I couldn't have been any more surprised. Or hurt. Or humiliated.

I had been used. And I couldn't do a single thing about it. Everything in me wanted to throw that blasted money on the floor and stomp out of there.

But I couldn't. I knew what white people said about "smart niggers." I knew better than to be one of those.

I shuffled off that back porch, head down—ashamed, degraded, violated. I didn't want anyone to know I had been exploited. I hated myself.

God does not want any of us to endure such loss of dignity and self-respect. He sent His Son into the world not to condemn us, but to give us new identity as His sons and daughters. God wills for us to accept His adoption whereby we become "heirs of God and fellow-heirs with Christ" (Rom. 8:17).

There are discoveries to be made about ourselves, when we are in a right relationship with God, which will make us spiritually healthy. Not the least of these discoveries is the good news that we are accepted even though we are unacceptable. When the Prophet Isaiah went up into the temple to pray, in the year that King Uzziah died, he discovered that his sin made him unacceptable. Overwhelmed by a vision of the glorious presence of God, he responded: "Woe is me! for I am undone; because I am a man of unclean lips, and I dwell in the midst of a people of unclean lips; for mine eyes have seen the King, the Lord of hosts" (Isa. 6:5, KJV).

While Isaiah realized his own inadequacies and unacceptableness, he also discovered the grace of God which made him acceptable. God provided cleansing from his sinfulness when an angel was sent to purge him: "Then flew one of the seraphims unto me, having a live coal in his hand, which he had taken with the tongs from off the altar: and he laid it upon my mouth, and said, 'Lo, this has touched thy lips; and thine iniquity is taken away, and thy sin purged' " (Isa. 6:6-7, KJV).

Lastly, Isaiah learned that God had a mission for him that gave his life ultimate significance: "Also I heard the voice of the Lord, saying, 'Whom shall I send, and who will go for Us?'

Then said I, 'Here am I; send me' " (Isa. 6:8).

Therein lies the basis on which each of us can gain a wholesome sense of selfhood. Like Isaiah, we must be humbled with the discovery that our sinfulness has rendered us unacceptable to a holy God; but through the grace of God, we learn the amazing news that He makes us acceptable and gives to each of us a significant mission in life. When we grasp what we are apart from Christ, we are stripped of our pride; and when we realize that because He still loves us, He purges our sin and gives to each of us special gifts in order to carry out His calling for us, our dignity is established.

My pastor told this story from his boyhood. He came home from school one day in tears, threw himself into his mother's lap, and cried, "Mamma, am I a nigger?" His mother asked firmly, as only a black mother can, "Who told you you're a nigger?"

"The kids down at school, they told me I'm a nigger."

"Listen," said his mother, "you're a nigger when I tell you you're a nigger—and I never will."

Whenever the people around us attempt to degrade us, we must remember what God says we are. He calls us to a high calling and gives us a title that clothes us with dignity.

Once a friend of mine encountered a little girl carrying a huge mass of cotton candy on a paper cone. He asked, "How can a little girl like you eat all of that cotton candy?"

"Well you see, Mister," the little girl answered, "I'm really much bigger on the inside than I am on the outside."

Pride leads us to pretend to be bigger on the outside than we are on the inside. Healthy humility is the recognition that God has imparted to each of us, by His grace, a gift which makes us greater on the inside than most people will ever know.

CHAPTER FIVE

ENVY

THE PLAY *Amadeus* was praised by the critics. The movie made from the play won an Academy Award. Both the play and the movie brilliantly carried us into the subjective consciousness of a good man who was destroyed by envy. Antonio Salieri, court musician to the King of Austria in Vienna, encountered the teenage musical genius, Wolfgang Amadeus Mozart. Young Mozart was obviously blessed with talents which set him apart from his contemporaries. His virtuosity on the harpsichord was dazzling. His music was complex, moving, exciting, and reflected his total mastery of virtually all forms of composition. It was clear that God had endowed him with extraordinary gifts. Nevertheless Mozart was immature, vulgar, obscene and lascivious.

Salieri, on the other hand, had dedicated himself to serving God, promising to write music that would glorify the Heavenly Father. From his youth he had dreamed of composing music that would lift the hearts of people heavenward. Salieri was committed to serving God and asked only that God might permit him to create the kind of music that would reflect His glory. However, God had not endowed Salieri with such gifts. Salieri was able to write pleasant tunes, but not masterpieces. He could compose music which would entertain its hearers, but never immortalize its composer. Despite his immense popularity, Salieri knew that his was a mediocre talent and that his uninspired work would soon be forgotten. Because he envied Mozart's gifts, he violated the commandment against covetousness and became obsessed with envy which led him to plot Mozart's destruction. This obsession eventually drove him to insanity. In the climatic monologue of the play, Salieri curses God for denying him the kind of talent which He granted to Mozart. In this play we see a brilliant illustration of how envy can alienate a person from God.

ENVY DEFINED

Envy is a desire to have what another person has. It is not simply a longing to have the same kind of thing the other person has; the envious person wants to strip another of something in order to possess it completely and solely.

I know of an athlete who for years was the darling of his fans. When his name was announced, the crowds in the stands would go wild with cheering. He stood apart from the other members of the team, not only for his athletic ability, but also because of his personal style. He was the epitomy of graciousness. People referred to him as "classy" and the adjective aptly described him.

Then one season a rookie showed up at training camp. There was something almost charismatic about this young man which immediately attracted the attention of the press. He played with a flair and demonstrated an awesome talent which little by little gained the attention of the crowds. Soon the cries of adulation for him began to rival those give to the veteran player.

Now the older man is slowing down and only occasionally shows flashes of his former greatness. The presence of the newcomer presents a great challenge to the tired veteran. He can gracefully move out of the limelight giving way to the new idol; he can become a mentor to the younger player, teaching him the lifestyle which could earn him the respect of the community. Or, the veteran can allow himself to be eaten up with envy and lose his "class." He can become irritated by the "hot-dogging" antics of the younger man and make disparaging remarks to the press about the rookie which would reveal pettiness and bitterness. The final chapter of this sports drama is still waiting to be lived out. The veteran's admirers are hoping for the best.

ENVY IN THE CHURCH

Envy expresses itself in all walks of life. Its presence is evident even within church vocations. Too often preachers, missionaries and church and denominational leaders, supposedly committed to presenting Christ, allow themselves to be consumed by envy.

In a rural community in New Jersey, there are three struggling churches. One of these churches secured a new dynamic pastor whose gifts for preaching far exceeded the gifts of the other two pastors in town. The new man immediately attracted the attention and the admiration of the community. It seemed that everybody was buzzing about how good his sermons were. This new preacher drew large crowds for his Sunday services and his congregation soon included new members who used to belong to the other two churches.

As the obvious superiority of the new preacher became increasingly evident, so did the envy of the other two pastors. It was not long before that envy was translated into malicious behavior. The two rival preachers took every opportunity to compare his style of ministry with their own, making it clear that they deemed their less flamboyant ways to be truer expressions of Christianity. They claimed that the large crowds the new preacher attracted could be attributed to the fact that he preached what people wanted to hear instead of the Gospel. That was only the beginning of their evil. When they heard of some unfounded rumors about possible sexual indiscretions by their rival, they fed these rumors with innuendos and knowing glances.

Envy often leads people to lie, because the envious are capable of using almost any means possible to destroy their rivals. While in this case the two envious preachers did not lie, they did feed the rumors which were floating around town. It was not long before the reputation of the new preacher was called into question. As the stories spread, this young man became increasingly tenuous in his sermons and the fire which had characterized his delivery was gone. Because of the envy of his colleagues, he was eventually discredited and he found it impossible to continue his ministry in that community. The envy of those two men not only destroyed the ministry of an effective pastor, but eventually they made themselves appear so petty and mean in the eyes of the townspeople that their own ministries were significantly damaged.

ENVY IN THE WORLD

The television fare of any season offers numerous opportunities to view a variety of beauty pageants. From Miss America to Miss Universe, we can see paraded before us on our television screens a seemingly endless array of women vying with each other for coveted crowns. When the winners of such contests are announced, the other contestants generally gather around the designated beauty queens and smother them with kisses. The losers pretend to be happy for the winners as they smile for the audience and the cameras, but there are hints in their demeanor that many of these losers would just as soon see the winners drop dead. Often their body language reveals an envy which they are doing their utmost to conceal.

Recently, a shocking story of the horrible consequences which can result from envy appeared in the national press. The story covered the murder of an attractive teenager from a California high school. The all-American girl had tried out for the cheerleading team and had won a place among that elite group which to many exemplifies what it means to be an adorable teenager. The cheerleaders in her particular school were elected by the student body. To win a position on the team was tantamount to being designated as among the cutest and most popular girls on the campus.

Unfortunately, such contests inevitably leave behind a string of losers. Among the losers of this election was a girl whose envy had no limits. This rejected teenager had lost out to a rival of long standing who time and time again had won the recognition she craved. Her envy got the best of her. Eventually she murdered her competitor, and was able to take her position on the cheerleading team. When the tragic truth was finally discovered, emotional shock waves ran through the school and the community. The incident clearly demonstrated the extremes to which a young person could go in pursuit of glamor and popularity.

Jewish folklore has many stories which depict the ugliness of envy. One of the most intriguing is about a certain store owner who was visited by an angel. The angel offered the man a wish that would give him anything he desired. However, there was one condition—his rival, whom he envied intensely, would receive double what the wish granted. Without hesitation, the envious man wished to be blind in one eye.

The Bible abounds with examples of envy and its dire consequences. The slaying of Abel by Cain resulted from Cain envying the favor which Abel gained in the eyes of God. The plans of Saul to kill David resulted from Saul's envy of David's popularity. According to the biblical tradition, envy is what caused the fall of Satan. The Bible gives ample evidence of the fact that envy is the cause of some of our greatest sins.

WANTING TO BE ENVIED

Most people enjoy being envied and work hard at encouraging others to envy them. This desire to encourage envy is clearly apparent among children. Most of us can recall examples from our childhood which illustrate this tendency. Few things tempted me to lie more than the desire to be envied. When the other kids who lived in my neighborhood returned to school after a summer filled with great vacations and exciting trips, I felt some kind of urge to make up stories about what I did during the summer. My invented tales made their true reports seem pale by comparison and I, who envied them their good fortune, would end up having them envy me. Every youngster knows that it is more fun to be the one envied than to be the envier.

My son, Bart, has a best friend named John. Their relationship goes all the way back to the early days of their childhood. It was fascinating to watch the two boys interact over the years. They seemed to spend much of their time doing their best to elicit each other's envy. If John had some special toy, he gained great satisfaction from making Bart envious by convincing him that there was no toy in his collection which was comparable. In response, Bart dreamed of possessing things which would make John envious. At times this competitive relationship created bad feelings between them and resulted in months of alienation. I am convinced that if it had not been for their conversions to Christ, these two boys never would have maintained the relationship which blossomed into the great friendship they share today. It was the transformation of their thinking and their subsequent commitment to a biblically prescribed lifestyle that saved them from destroying their friendship.

The psychological fulfillment which comes from being envied is sought not only by children. A great deal of adult behavior is generated by the desire for this same kind of gratification. Thorstein Veblen, one of America's most brilliant economic theorists, claims that the spending habits of people are highly influenced by the psychic enjoyment which comes from getting others to long for what they possess. It is Veblen's contention that it is possible to get people to buy products that are not particularly superior in quality, by publicizing widely that the products are *very* expensive. This practice which Veblen calls *conspicuous consumption*, motivates people to buy expensive automobiles because the buyers know that most other people in the society know that these cars are very expensive. Veblen claims that people buy costly items not necessarily because they are better in quality, but because their possession displays to others how rich the owners are. The fact that expensive possessions stimulate the envy of those who do not have them and gives great satisfaction to those who do have them.

Veblen believes that this principle of envy extends even to marriage. He claims that some people, usually men, choose their mates more to be the envy of their peers than as partners who will share their love. There are some who turn away from loving relationships because their prospective partners will not elicit the envy of others. I know of one man who was engaged to a fine woman but refused to marry her because he knew that his friends would not be impressed by her appearance. She shared his interests and was a stimulating conversationalist. They had similar values and held the same Christian convictions. Nevertheless, he married another woman who had striking beauty, but few of the sterling qualities of his former fiancé. He lost out on an opportunity that would have brought him significant happiness because it was more important to him to have a wife who would make him the envy of others than one who would make him happy.

Some men, according to Veblen, encourage their wives to spend large amounts of money on clothes and home furnishings simply to advertise the fact that they can afford such things. It takes so much time to earn money that these men don't have time to acquire the things which will conspicuously display their wealth. Consequently, they use their wives to buy those items which will cause others to envy their success. Their wives may not view themselves as being used and they may even think that their husbands' generosity is an expression of love. However, what lies behind such subtle exploitation is the desire to be envied.

ENVY AND WOMEN

In our sexist culture, women are often manipulated into the painful position of envying each other. The values of our society make it difficult for women who are older or less attractive not to envy those who are young, slim, and beautiful. Our cultural conditioning frequently makes them feel that they have lost much of their worth simply because they lack the stereotypical requisites for attractiveness.

The status of married women is still often determined by their husbands. Some marry men with prestige in order to be the envy of others. Those who fail to marry well often envy those who do. Women can cause their husbands pain by comparing them unfavorably with the husbands of their friends. Such comparisons can generate bitterness and pain in wives as well, if they nurture their belief that they deserved better than they got.

Frequently women who enjoy being envied by their friends unwittingly alienate them by bragging about all the wonderful things they possess and by providing incredible reports of how well their children are doing. Those who have to listen to these often exaggerated tales may feel that they are being indirectly criticized. Such attempts to generate envy often produce nothing more than irritation and resentment.

The desire to be the envy of others by surpassing them in possessions often leads to overspending and consequently to marital conflict. It is not surprising that disagreement over money is the most often cited cause for divorce.

Robert and Helen Lynds conducted what many sociologists consider to be the classic study of Middle America when they analyzed the behavior of people in Muncie, Indiana. The Lynds found that the working people of Muncie purchased a host of household gadgets and appliances to gain status in the community. They were willing to work extra hours and forgo precious time of shared family life to buy these things. Often women took jobs, even though they preferred to be home with their children, because they wanted to have money to buy those things which would make them the envy of others. Thus, envy contributed to the weakening of family life in Muncie.

ENVY IS DESTRUCTIVE

There is little doubt in the minds of those who observe human interaction closely that envy is a major cause of unhappiness and self-contempt. Those who envy are never happy with what they are and have. They hate themselves for not being the persons they envy and despise themselves for not possessing what the envied possess.

Malcolm X, the murdered leader of the black people of Harlem during the 1960s, wrote of how his envy of white people almost destroyed him psychologically. In a social system which had made things so difficult for him and his black brothers and sisters, he envied the advantages enjoyed by whites. He so much wanted to be white and have what whites had that he went to great lengths to reject his own black identity. Malcolm X explained how he purchased special skin creams which promised to lighten the color of the skin. He described his willingness to burn his scalp with a hot hair-straightening iron that would remove the kinkiness of natural black hair and make it more like the hair of the envied whites. His envy led him to hate white people for having what he wanted. His autobiography tells the story of how he was able to work through his destructive envy and overcome his hatred of himself and of white people.

Malcolm X makes it clear that the freedom of black people will not be secured simply by gaining the political and economic opportunities enjoyed by whites. Black people, he argues, must stop envying white people and stop trying to *be* white. He wanted black people to be able to say with conviction, "Black is beautiful." Only when black people are free from envying white people and all that goes with whiteness, and start to glory in what they themselves are, will freedom from the tyranny of whites ever be possible.

The man who covets another man's wife becomes discontented with his own. The student who envies another student's grades underestimates his own abilities. The woman who envies another woman's sexy appearance becomes a supporter of a cultural system which diminishes her own value and encourages her own unhappiness.

Envy diminishes people's enjoyment of life because they cannot be content with what they possess. In the story of The Prodigal Son (Luke 15), the older brother envies the love which his father bestows on his wayward younger brother. Because his envy makes him bitter, he loses out on the opportunity to enjoy a happy celebration, and fails to appreciate all that his father has and feels for him.

There was a married couple in one of the churches I served who had a lovely son. The boy was both gentle and kind. In so many ways he was Christlike in demeanor. However, this young man lacked both the intelligence and talents to become a professional person. His parents wanted him to be a doctor or a lawyer, but he was destined to be a manual worker. Instead of enjoying a wonderful son who was a blessing wherever he went, they envied their friends who had children in more prestigious vocations. The young man was able to rise above the negative attitude of his parents and live a happy life, but they lost out on the opportunity to enjoy and be proud of a very special son. These parents went through life feeling cheated, instead of appreciating the wonderful gift which God had given them.

OVERCOMING ENVY

The first thing to bear in mind, in your effort to overcome envy, is that God wills the very best for you. I am not suggesting that what God wants is always realized. If such were the case, there would be no sin in the world. But if you are to rid yourself of resentment against God, it is crucial that you grasp the wonderful truth that God has meant for you to serve an infinitely important role in His kingdom, and that He has willed for you to have the gifts and opportunities to live out that role. In short, whatever you *think* you lack is not God's fault. He willed the best for you because His love for you knows no limits. There may have been evil factors and personal sin interfering with the *initial* will of God. What you have done, or what others have done, may have thwarted His will so that the good things He willed for you have not materialized; but remember, God is a good God who wills for you all of those gifts and attributes essential for you to live your life in the fullness of joy.

The good news of the Gospel is that God cannot be stopped. The good that He willed for each of us from before the foundation of the earth *will* come to pass in God's eternal kingdom. The blockage of His intentions is only apparent and temporary. Eventually the good that He wills for us will be realized. Regardless of the frustrations and barriers we encounter, we have this wonderful assurance: "And we know that in everything God works for good with those who love Him, who are called according to His purpose" (Rom. 8:28). Part of that fulfillment is during our earthly lives, and part of it in heaven.

Instead of being resentful and envying those for whom things seem to have turned out better, we are called to trust God and to believe that in the midst of our present circumstances, He will find a way of providing opportunities for each of us to experience joyful service and total fulfillment regardless of the difficult conditions or deprivations which we have had to endure.

In his book, *The Will of God,* Leslie Weatherhead says that we should all be searching for the possibilities which exist in our lives. He tells us that if we do, we can discover the significant and sometimes amazing opportunities for good which He has waiting for us in even the worst of situations.

I know of no better contemporary example of this than Joni

Eareckson Tada. This incredible, vivacious young woman became a quadriplegic as the result of a diving accident. A life of sports, travel, and fun seemed to be over. The promise of a professional career and a happy marriage appeared to be gone. She was confined to a wheelchair for life instead of being free to live the happy life which she had anticipated for herself.

As Joni tells her story, she explains how easy it would have been for her to envy others who were able-bodied, and how envy could have made her into a bitter person. It is a wonder that envy and resentment did not distort her personality. Instead, by the grace of God, Joni discovered some truths that changed her life.

First of all, she came to recognize that what had happened was not something that God wanted to happen. She realized that God did not want her to suffer and to be crippled for life. She came to see that Satan wanted to use her tragic accident to cause her to hate God, but she was determined not to let Satan have his way. She affirmed the biblical message that God is good and wills only good for His children. Once she realized that God did not will her accident, and that He suffered with her as she had to live with its consequences, she found it easier to love God and worship Him.

Secondly, Joni discovered that in the midst of the difficult circumstances in which she found herself, God could give her meaning and joy. She discovered that *because* of the horrible thing which had happened to her, she was equipped to minister to other handicapped persons in a way that is impossible for those who are not disabled. Even though God did not will her to be crippled, He could work in the midst of her adversity to produce something of infinite importance.

Seeing how God could use her because of her condition became a source of joy; and her testimony, now heard around the world, has influenced countless persons.

Joni is still a young woman. The end of her story remains to be told. Her struggle to overcome frustration and envy will continue for a lifetime, but I have confidence in her ability to conquer those feelings, because I know that she is nurturing her relationship with God.

She lives in the hope that someday, all the good things which God willed for her from before her birth will come to pass. That is what heaven is for and Joni knows it. She is able to use as a weapon against envy the knowledge that eventually she will lack for nothing that is good. She knows that someday she will walk again, even if that someday is in heaven.

WISDOM CONQUERS ENVY

I heard of an Oriental man who visited America. This guest in our country had come to study pieces of Chinese art which by one means or another had been taken out of his country and brought to ours. He loved art as only a true connoisseur can. Each artifact, vase, statue, and painting that he saw evoked his deep appreciation.

One day this gentleman was invited to the home of one of the richest art collectors in America to see all of the magnificent examples of Chinese art in the collection. At one point during the visit, the American collector took from his safe a crystal ball which had belonged to one of the emperors of the Ming Dynasty. When this breathtaking piece of art was shown to the oriental visitor, his response was, "Thank you for keeping this for me. I am indebted to you for all you have done to make it possible for me to enjoy this crystal ball." When the American asked what his guest meant by this statement, the man from China answered, "Is it not true that the beauty of this crystal ball is just as available for me to enjoy as it is for you? Yet I did not have to bear the expense of purchasing it or the cost of keeping it safe."

"That is true," answered the American collector, "but you do not have the joy of owning it."

"Why should I envy you for owning it if it can offer you no more beauty than it offers me? Furthermore, you do not own it. It was in the hands of someone else before you were born and it will be in the hands of still another after you are dead. It is for you to take care of this beautiful thing while you are still alive and to share its beauty with any who ask to see it. Is it not true that if I should come again, you would show it to me and allow me to enjoy its beauty again? Then why should I envy you for having this crystal ball?"

The wisdom and logic of the visitor's argument are clear and indisputable. It is this kind of wisdom which is an effective antidote for envy.

In the Taoist literature of ancient China is a story that demonstrates how foolish envy really is. It seems that there was a wise man who had many wonderful horses. There was one horse which was so strong, fast, and beautiful that it elicited the envy of the man's neighbor. However, one day this horse escaped from the barn and ran away into the hills. The neighbor's envy changed to pity, but the wise man said, "Who knows if I should be pitied or if I should be envied because of this?"

The next day the horse returned to the wise man leading a herd of fifty equally beautiful wild horses with him. The neighbor once again was filled with envy and once again the wise man said, "Who knows if I should be envied or if I should be pitied because of this?" Shortly after he said this, his only son tried to ride one of the wild horses, fell off of it and broke his right leg. The neighbor's envy once again turned to pity, but the wise man responded by saying, "Who knows if I should be pitied or if I should be envied because of this?"

The next day the general of the emperor's army came to draft the man's son for an exceedingly dangerous mission, but since the son's leg was broken, he could not be recruited for this mission which promised certain death. The neighbor, whose own son was taken in the place of the injured young man, envied the wise man; and once again the wise man said, "Who know if I should be envied or pitied because of this?"

The story goes on and on with similar twists that shift the neighbor's feelings from envy to pity and then back to envy again. But the wisdom of this man makes it clear that things are not always what they seem to be, and that what we desire is as likely to bring us pain and trouble as satisfaction and good fortune.

How many times have we seen people destroyed by the very traits we admire and perhaps covet? How often do we encounter people who are too attractive for their own good or so talented that they never learn the discipline of hard work and persistence? How often do we see people destroyed by the riches that made them the envy of others?

The great American poet Edwin Arlington Robinson brilliantly illustrates the futility of envy in the brief dramatic poem "Richard Cory."

> Whenever Richard Cory went down town,
> We people on the pavement looked at him;
> He was a gentleman from sole to crown,
> Clean favored, and imperially slim.
>
> And he was always quietly arrayed,
> And he was always human when he talked;
> But still he fluttered pulses when he said,
> "Good morning," and he glittered when he walked.
>
> And he was rich—yes, richer than a king—
> And admirably schooled in every grace;
> In fine, we thought that he was everything
> To make us wish that we were in his place.
>
> So on we worked, and waited for the light,
> And went without the meat, and cursed the bread;
> And Richard Cory, one calm summer night,
> Went home and put a bullet through his head.

Richard Cory, handsome, wealthy and gracious, a man who was envied by all who knew him, was also a troubled and lonely man whose pain could not be relieved by his money. Those things that people envied him were hollow and without substance.

We all need wisdom to handle what we have and to view properly what others have. God is the giver of such wisdom. "But if ye have bitter jealousy and selfish ambition in your hearts, do not boast and be false to the truth" (James 3:14).

Last, but by no means least, giving thanks for what we already possess can deliver us from envy of those who have what we yearn for. Giving thanks is wonderful therapy for envy. My wife uses this remedy with great success and I attribute her optimism and contentment to her ability to see the positive aspects of her circumstances, whatever they may be. If we miss an airplane and have to wait two hours for the next one, she looks upon the two-hour wait as a gift from God so that the two of us can have this uninterrupted time to visit with each other. If I go out in the morning and find that my car battery is dead, she tells me how lucky I am that I did not have this trouble when I was out on some deserted highway. If my coat gets ripped, she welcomes the opportunity to buy a new one.

She always considers herself to be a most fortunate person and she lets if be known that she would not want to be anyone else or have any other children than her own; and, strange as it seems to me, she considers it her good fortune to have me for a husband. Now I ask you, how can I not love a woman like that?

When I asked her if she ever felt that the grass was greener on the other side of the fence, she answered, "If you think that the grass is greener on the other side of the fence, it is probably because you are not properly caring for the grass on your own side." If each of us would care for and appreciate the possibilities in what we have, we would cease to envy what others have.

The Apostle Paul said that love does not envy anyone. Loving those whom God has given us to love, enjoying what

God has given us to enjoy, and taking advantage of the opportunities God has provided can be a reliable remedy for envy. This word to the wise should be sufficient.

CHAPTER SIX
GLUTTONY

OF THE SERMONS I wish I had never preached, none elicits more regret than a sermon on the subject of gluttony. It was delivered at a Bible conference in Maryland where I regularly speak. As I prepared for this particular occasion, I thought about the fact that we preachers too often admonish against the sins of those who are not in our audiences and seldom touch upon those sins of which our listeners are most likely to be guilty. I decided to break from that tendency and attack a sin which was all too evident among these otherwise godly people. I decided to preach against overeating. I reasoned that there were not many adulterers, thieves, and liars in the audience; but I knew by the looks of many of them that gluttony was a common sin.

In retrospect, I regret preaching that sermon, not because I believe that sins should not be boldly condemned, but because the public condemnation of gluttony is an unfair and cruel thing to do. The cruelty was not apparent to me at the time. When I preached the sermon, I was convinced that the obesity of those in the congregation was due to a lack of willpower on their part and a decision to let themselves go physically. I figured that most people enjoy eating and that these fat people simply did not see that it was wrong to overdo it. I was unaware back then that most obese people despise their fatness and suffer emotionally because of their tendency to overeat. I had no understanding of the complex factors contributing to a problem which afflicts so many.

CHEMICAL IMBALANCE

Some of my friends who are well-read on the subject of nutrition have convinced me that many overweight people are food addicts and have little control over their insatiable desire to overeat. Most fat people are hooked on food in much the same way that cocaine or heroin addicts are hooked on drugs. There is something terribly wrong with their physiological makeup that drives them to eat, much as alcoholics are driven to drink. The experts tell us that obese people often suffer from some chemical imbalance that creates a craving for food. In most instances, the food which is craved is actually harmful to the individual, and aggravates the chemical imbalance which is responsible for their overeating in the first place.

A very fat seminary graduate took over the pastorate of a small rural church I had served while a graduate student. The church was hardly an ecclesiastical plum, but it was the best that this young man could get. As is often the case, his weight had caused him to be rejected by several to which he applied for consideration. He was perceived as a jolly happy-go-lucky sort of guy who would be a good Santa at a Christmas party, but hardly the type to properly represent a church which wanted to be taken seriously in its community. He settled for this student charge and was glad that anybody at all was willing to accept him as pastor.

This new pastor proved to be a wonderful servant of God and a man who deeply loved the members of his church. Although he would have liked to be married, the fact that he was single enabled him to give all of his time to serving the needs of his congregation. The youth of the church enjoyed him, as he seemed to be a good sport about their jokes and jabs about his weight.

Then one Sunday morning in the middle of his sermon, to the shock of his audience, this overweight preacher collapsed and fell to the floor unconscious. He was hospitalized and listed in serious condition. After a battery of tests, the doctors announced their diagnosis: he was suffering from malnutrition. Hardly anyone in the church could believe the news. "How," they asked one another, "could he be malnourished? He eats more than any of us. He never passes up seconds at a church supper and he's always ready for cookies and cake."

What they did not know was that many people are over-weight because their diets are unbalanced so that certain essential minerals and vitamins are missing. The absence of certain nutrients can create a chemical imbalance which makes people crave foods which are devoid of the things their bodies really need. Because their diets do not meet their physical needs, when they have finished consuming a normal amount of food, they still crave more. In his book *Overfed But Under-nourished*, Dr. H. Curtis Wood, Jr. describes this condition as "hidden hunger," an abnormal craving for food, caused by a diet that is inadequate and lacking in certain elements the body needs" (p. 178).

In some instances, overweight people may even have an aversion to those foods which might help to bring their body chemistry back into balance. In extreme cases, the victims of malnutrition have been known to develop *pica*. The victim suffering from pica may long to eat things which are not even food. For instance, some malnourished pregnant women have an intense desire to eat starch. This may also explain why some children eat such unappealing nonfood substances as paint chips.

Autistic children also evidence appetite abnormalities. It appears that many autistic children suffer from chemical im-balance and that they frequently have been known to want to eat only one type of food, such as hamburgers or peanut butter. Others eat large quantities of one food at a time without regard to their need for nutritional balance. In con-tinuing to eat improperly, their already abnormal nervous systems are further damaged.

Nutritional scientists have not reached agreement on the causes of the chemical imbalances that create insatiable cravings for the wrong food in obese people; but Dr. Lendon

Smith, a pediatrician well known for his work in nutrition, and some of his colleagues believe that a strong craving for a particular food often indicates an allergy to that food. Some think that these problems can be traced to genetic factors. Still others argue that this condition may be generated from over-eating in early childhood.

Too many parents think that a plump child is a healthy child. They attempt to show love by coaxing their children to overeat. Such parents often do not realize that they may be creating an unhealthy condition in their children, that wrong eating habits can lead to chemical imbalance. Furthermore, there is general agreement that children who become fat in their early years are likely to be battling a weight problem for the rest of their lives. Once the body adjusts to fatness as a normal condition, the metabolism of the body operates so as to maintain that condition throughout life. Since a predisposition to obesity can result from genetics, from parental error, or from disease, there is little question that the imbalances in body chemistry which lead to obesity are not necessarily the result of willful decisions on the part of its victims.

In the light of these findings, it is easy to understand why I later felt guilty about my sermon condemning fat people for their condition. What was even worse was that they were so visible. Adulterers do not publicly declare their sin by their physical appearance. Liars cannot be detected by looking at them. Thieves look like the rest of us. But those who are overweight are visible and are immediately assumed to be gluttonous by everyone they meet. There is no concealing their problem.

My sermon was particularly cruel because it left "the guilty" exposed with no place to hide. It is wrong to publicly condemn people who should be confronted in private. There is little justification for the humiliation which so many must suffer at the hands of insensitive and uninformed preachers who like to wax prophetic at the expense of people who are already suffering in ways that are not readily understood.

DIET PROGRAMS

This sympathetic statement on behalf of fat people should not be taken as a justification for overeating. There is a difference between an explanation and a justification. What I have presented has been an attempt at the former, rather than the latter. The Bible condemns gluttony. In the book of Proverbs we read, "Be not among winebibbers, or among gluttonous eaters of meat; for the drunkard and the glutton will come to poverty, and drowsiness will clothe a man with rags (Prov. 23:21-11). Plato defined a good person as one whose appetites are under the control of his will and whose will is under the control of the mind.

To those who do not have a weight problem, controlling one's eating habits is not as easy as it appears. The array of commercial products promising easy solutions to this extremely difficult malady offer relatively little help. Pharmaceutical companies promise that their products will facilitate weight loss; publishers promise that their books will help to solve the problem; and there are psychoanalysts who invite fat people to spend a small fortune in order to unravel the deep-seated causes of their gluttony. Few of these promises are realized. None of the quick answers work. The psychotherapeutic treatments seldom provide any lasting effects. It breaks my heart to see fat people try so hard and achieve so little from the various methods they employ to lose weight. It is sad to watch people driven to despair as they fail to get rid of the fat that is making their lives miserable.

The commercialism surrounding weight loss also has found a home in the religious community. There are Christian organizations which call on fat people to lose weight for the glory of God. Christian music companies sell records and tapes with such religious titles as *Building a Firm Foundation* as they make exercising off undesirable pounds a spiritual calling. Consequently, those who fail to lose weight are made to feel even greater pangs of guilt as they sense that they have disappointed God.

A local television station decided to feature a series of programs on weight reduction in which an overweight person would go through the routines suggested by the diet and exercise expert who was the star of an early morning show. This woman was to do all the things the expert told her to do. She was to eat the right foods, limit her calorie intake and exercise properly in accord with his directions.

The producers of the show were hopeful that with each weekly appearance of this "example" of how obesity could be conquered, visible progress could be demonstrated. Those at the TV station were convinced that it would make for great viewing to watch the week-by-week transformation of a 200-pound woman into a "shapely knockout."

Unfortunately, the experiment failed. At first the woman demonstrated dramatic progress. The loss of the first ten pound occurred in a couple of weeks. The expert was euphoric with this public demonstration of the success of his methods. The Neilson ratings of the show improved significantly. Then something very sad happened; progress stopped abruptly. The woman gradually regained the lost weight. The station decided to take the demonstration off the air.

The failure of this woman was caused by a variety of factors, but none was more significant than the fact that obesity cannot be conquered by a person who does not stick to the regimen twenty-four hours a day. After losing a few pounds through austere discipline, this woman felt she was entitled to a few pieces of candy as a reward. When nobody was watching, she sneaked some hamburgers and french fries at a fast-food outlet. Whenever she violated the prescribed routine, she assured herself that she would do better tomorrow. But she could not control herself and she cheated.

Most people who set out to lose weight are much the same. My mother, who by no means could have been considered obese, decided to take off a few of her extra pounds by joining Weight Watchers, an organization which uses some of the techniques of Alcoholics Anonymous to help fat people to deal with their problem. The group met weekly so that its members could testify to their progress. My mother's group had a good time together. They enjoyed good-natured fun and a lot of jokes. My mother lost very little weight as a result of her participation in the group, but she continued to go to the weekly meetings because they gave her so much pleasure. If she did demonstrate any weight loss at the weigh-in which was part of each meeting, she and her friends would later go out to celebrate by enjoying hot-fudge sundaes. A good time was had by all, but not too much was accomplished as far as weight loss was concerned.

The Weight Watchers approach is by no means in error. It simply does not go far enough. Their imitation of the techniques of Alcoholics Anonymous would be a good idea if only it were carried out with thoroughness. A.A. assumes that its members will be facing constant struggles with their alcohol problems and require a round-the-clock support system. Members of A.A. are committed to helping each other morning, noon, and night. Any member who feels that the temptation to indulge in some of the old drinking pleasures knows that help is only a phone call away. There is always someone who is willing to drop everything and rush to the side of the suffering alcoholic during the immediate period of travail. Those who are in A.A. must admit that they are alcoholics and that physiological factors generate within them a craving for alcohol that is too intense to be controlled by their own willpower. Members of A.A. acknowledge a need for one another's support to overcome their alcoholism. Furthermore, they know that they will always be alcoholics, that they will always have desperate longings to drink, that they will be in a state of dependency on others for support, and that without supernatural help they will not be able to stay sober. It is this stark realism about the problem of alcohol which is the basis of the success of this organization. Those who deal with the problem of obesity must be just as serious about it as A.A. is about alcoholism.

NEED FOR SUPPORT

Overweight people have a chronic problem which cannot be solved independently. Those who make a decision to lose weight are unlikely to achieve their goal unless they are surrounded by persons who are willing to keep tabs on them daily and to be available to support them at a moment's notice. This affords the church a chance to fly its colors of love for all the world to see. A Christian fellowship can undertake the nurturing of its overweight people as perhaps no other group can. It can encourage obese members to conquer the problem by committing itself to work with the suffering persons.

This entails much more than providing periodic words of encouragement. It requires that assigned members of the church check constantly to make sure that the obese person sticks to the prescribed diet. It necessitates being available around the clock to go to the side of the sufferer when temptation becomes too great to withstand. It demands a willingness to pray with that person regularly and to be ready to kneel before the Lord seeking help in hours of need.

Such constant care is not something that can be provided for a period of months and then abandoned when the weight problem seems to be under control. There must be a recognition of the fact that the problem will never be conquered completely. The tendency to "pig out" after victories in weight loss are all too common. The temptation to gluttony will be forever present in one who has been obese.

Victory over the temptation to be gluttonous is achieved one day at a time, and only with the help of God and the support system of brothers and sisters who love enough to give significant amounts of time to winning those victories. The Apostle Paul instructed us to "bear one another's burdens and so fulfill the law of Christ" (Gal. 6:2). Providing a support system for overweight people who are tortured by their obesity is one way in which Christians can live out that biblical command.

There are those who argue that there are people in the Christian community who choose to be fat, and that it is wrong for us to necessarily consider skinniness as desirable. Gloria Vanderbilt once said that no woman can be too rich or too thin. Unfortunately, there is wide agreement with her in our society. We have defined beauty for women in such a way as to require something close to anorexia in order for them to comply with the requisites. The female models that dominate the media would have been considered gaunt and unhealthy by our Victorian forbears. Women who were considered sexually desirable, at another time in our history, would be considered grossly overweight by those who dictate the standards of female attractiveness today. Even Marilyn Monroe, the ultimate symbol of voluptuous female beauty twenty-five years ago, would be asked to go on a crash diet by the media masters of the 1980s.

Beauty, it is said, is in the eye of the beholder, and the beholders of contemporary society have given their thumbs down to the fat ladies unless they can sing. There are those who ask why we should call upon people to give up their gluttonous habits simply to conform to fetishes of the relativistic values of our culture. These proponents of a "live and let live" attitude toward fatness declare that weight is a matter of taste and we ought not to regard gluttony as something bad, let alone one of the seven deadly sins.

There is some merit in this defense of fat people, and it is a good thing, because the obese need all the help they can muster. There is widespread discrimination against overweight people that violates any canons of societal justice. Fat people are often refused employment opportunities because of their appearance. They are often left friendless by those who do not want to be seen with them.

While Christians must stand up for the civil rights of people and should be opposed to all forms of discrimination, they still must raise some important questions about obesity. First and foremost is the question of whether or not Christians have the right to abuse their bodies. The biblical doctrine that informs us that the body is the temple of God has particular relevance at this point:

> "All things are lawful for me," but not all things are helpful. "All things are lawful for me," but I will not be enslaved by anything. . . . Do you not know that your body is a temple of the Holy Spirit within you, which you have from God? You are not your own; you were bought with a price. So glorify God in your body (1 Cor. 6:12, 19-20).

Excess weight can increase susceptibility to diabetes and put a strain on the heart. It can foster a host of other diseases which include hypertension, orthopedic problems and psychological illness. People should maintain normal weight for reasons of health, and Christians should seek good health because spirituality requires that we take care of our bodies.

In a very real sense, because Christ dwells in each of us, what we suffer, He suffers. Our bodies are instruments through which He works in the world, and we must not do anything which would limit His work by impairing His instruments. Paul pleads with us to recognize that our bodies are not our own to be used according to our own whims.

> I appeal to you therefore, brethren, by the mercies of God, to present your bodies as a living sacrifice, holy and acceptable to God, which is your spiritual worship. Do not be conformed to this world, but be transformed by the renewal of your mind, that you may prove what is the will of God, what is good and acceptable and perfect (Rom. 12:1-2).

Furthermore, one's physical condition can influence spiritual well-being just as it does psychological health. Excessive consumption of sweets can create a "sugar high" which may be followed shortly by fatigue and lethargy or irritability. Our ability to live out our lives with joy is determined to some degree by our physical well-being. If we love people, we find it impossible to stand by quietly and watch them hurt themselves. We are constrained by love to encourage them to be the healthy people God wills for them to be, and we should be ready to make the sacrifices of time and energy which are necessary if we are to assist them in overcoming the urge to be gluttonous.

A few years ago Oral Roberts University captured some headlines when the leaders of this Christian institution announced that the members of their student body would be required to keep their weight under control. Students who were overweight were required to go on carefully prescribed diets and to adopt a strenuous program of physical exercise.

Many people criticized the leadership of the university for interfering in the private lives of the students. Yet, there is a consistency to these regulations. No evangelical Christian college would condone drunkenness or ignore drug abuse. Many theologically conservative schools do not allow smoking. Why then should gluttony and its resultant obesity be approved? If overeating is addictive, should not evangelical institutions seek to correct the abuses that result from this addiction as readily as they seek to curtail other abuses? Are not the leaders of Oral Roberts University exercising Christian love as they focus on the physical well-being of their students? Are not these academic leaders correct in calling for moderation in eating and thereby showing concern about the spiritual well-being of those in their academic community?

The Seventh Day Adventists have a great deal to say to the larger Christian community when it comes to recognizing that having a proper diet is a Christian responsibility. Ellen White, the founder of this movement, may be called into question on a variety of issues, but her teachings on diet were advanced for her time. Her suggestion that Christians should become vegetarians is not bad advice. Urging people to avoid eating things that are potentially harmful to health is consistent with biblical teaching and with common sense.

Those who are inclined to be critical of the seemingly extreme concern which Adventists show towards the diets of their members should consider the fact that most evangelical churches not only remain neutral and say little on this subject, but actually participate in the physical problems of many of their members. Altogether too often, church meetings are followed by refreshments which include cookies and the usual junk food such as pretzels and chips.

No thought is given to the fact that such things are temptations to those who are addicted to foods without nutritional value. We would not think of urging the alcoholic to drink a beer or two. We would not consider making drugs available to addicts. Nevertheless, we seldom consider the harm we do as we lay out tables full of refreshments before brothers and sisters who are struggling with food addiction. Many church gatherings are organized around suppers at which we often thoughtlessly encourage overeating. The Apostle Paul discussed the attitude of the Jews toward eating food that had been offered to idols:

> Food will not commend us to God. We are no worse off if we do not eat, and no better off if we do. Only take care lest this liberty of yours somehow become a stumbling block to the weak. For if any one sees you, a man of knowledge, at table in an idol's temple, might he not be encouraged, if his conscience is weak, to eat food offered to idols? And so by your knowledge this weak man is destroyed, the brother for whom Christ died.
>
> Thus, sinning against your brethren and wounding their conscience when it is weak, you sin against Christ. Therefore, if food is a cause of my brother's falling, I will never eat meat, lest I cause my brother to fall (1 Cor. 8:8-13).

In this passage, Paul admonishes us to avoid placing temptation in the way of our brothers and sisters and to be willing to relinquish some of our freedom for that reason. There is no excuse for churches to tempt overweight brothers and sisters to give in to their gluttonous tendencies. We are called upon to recognize the weaknesses of some of our members and to do nothing that would offend them or lead them into sin.

It is clear that most overweight people suffer from a poor self-image. Whether or not society is partially responsible for the self-loathing that is all too typical of overweight people is beside the point. Fat people often feel horrendous psychological pain over their physical appearance and experience significant unhappiness. Certainly, God does not will despondency. I know a man in his early thirties who confided in me how he felt about his obesity. This 300-pound man told me that at a New Year's Eve party he happened to get a glimpse of himself in a wall mirror. Sitting on a chair which seemed to be draped by his sagging body, he saw himself wearing one of those ridiculous pointed New Year's hats.

As midnight approached, he thought of the jokes people had made all evening at his expense. He thought of how he had pretended to play along with the painful cheap shots he had endured. None of the women at the party had sought his companionship even though he was alone, Everybody, he thought, regarded him as a merry buffoon, and as he saw his image in the mirror, the attitudes of the others at the party seemed justified. This sad fat man who covered up his hurt with jolly laughter told me that the only thing that kept him from killing himself that night was his fear of death and judgment. It is time that church people become sensitive to the suffering of their obese friends .

TOBACCO

In our modern society, there are many forms of addiction other than gluttony that are destructive to our physical and psychological well-being. Some people are addicted to alcohol, others to drugs, and still others to cigarettes. Then there is the "Christian drug" called coffee to which countless people are addicted and which many believe to be a contributing factor to some forms of cancer as well as to neurological and psychological disturbances. There are those drug addicts who abuse approved drugs which include pills to put them to sleep and pills to wake them up. Some take pills to quiet their nerves and pills to cut down stomach acid.

Substance abuse causes people to lose control over the intake of things which their bodies crave. Some people long continually for food; others desperately crave a variety of chemical substances that cause them far more harm than overeating. Paul tells the Philippians tearfully of those who "live as enemies of the cross of Christ," saying of them, that "Their end is destruction, their God is the belly, and they glory in their shame, with minds set on earthly things" (Phil. 3:18-19).

Consider cigarette addiction. We all know that smoking wreaks havoc upon health and may ultimately cause death, but there are millions of Americans who defy the warnings and keep on smoking. A recent study indicates that most smokers hate their addiction, but find it impossible to stop. Many of them have attempted to overcome this obnoxious habit to no avail. Like Mark Twain, each of them might say, "It's easy to stop smoking. I've done it dozens of times." Clearly those who are habitual smokers have areas of their lives which are not under the lordship of Christ.

I was brought up to believe that smoking was a sign that a person was not a Christian. The legalism of my home church prohibited smoking for anyone who wanted to have a good relationship with the Lord. However in the last two decades, we have loosened up on religious values and even have come to mock the practice of considering abstinence from smoking a mark of spirituality. Lately evangelicals have come to believe that the personal pieties which marked fundamentalist Christians in former times are simply "tribal rituals" which are culturally relative. Many of the more sophisticated brothers and sisters of the faith deliberately puff a pipe or cigarette to demonstrate their liberation from the so-called oppressive legalism of the past.

As I have watched this trend away from the earlier attitudes which condemned smoking, I have wondered if we are being foolish. We condemned cigarettes when there was no scientific evidence that smoking was related to health problems. Now that we know without question that it is one of the dominant causes of cancer and lung and heart diseases, we are becoming increasingly tolerant of smoking and its evils. In light of what the Surgeon General of the United States has to say about smoking, it seems to me that the church ought to be speaking out clearly against this addictive practice.

The economics of smoking has a significant influence on what the church has to say on the issue. In the South, there are areas in which the jobs of many church members are dependent on the cigarette industry. The churches in this region have tended to say very little against the tobacco industry out of fear of offending and losing many of their members. Furthermore, there are philanthropists who have made their fortunes in the tobacco industry. Several of these millionaire benefactors have endowed Christian colleges, financed seminaries, and endowed church programs. In light of these generous contributions by the wealthy merchants of cigarettes, the Christian community finds it difficult to speak out against the evil which they perpetrate.

Several years ago, I had a conversation with a young man who would admit to the title of hippie. As we sat together on a park bench, located along the Chicago lakefront, I tried to explain to him the evils of marijuana smoking. This hippie let me know in no uncertain terms that the government was hypocritical in its condemnation of marijuana smoking as long as it allowed cigarette smoking to go on undeterred. At one point, in our exchange, he shouted at me, "We all know why marijuana is illegal and tobacco is legal in this country. It's because there are billions of dollars behind the cigarette industry."

There was little I could say in response to his analysis. The tobacco industry spends vast amounts of money on lobbying for its interests. It contributes to the limit of the law as it finances the campaigns of political candidates who will support its interests. Because of all of these expenditures, the government has done very little to hinder the tobacco industry. Aside from requiring a fine print statement on cigarette packages and the elimination of television advertising, the people in Washington have failed to do anything about the seduction of people into this addictive habit. Money determines too much of the morality of government. Toleration of one of America's worst addictions continues.

Cigarette smoking harms not only the smokers but a host of others. Research indicates that nonsmokers in close proximity to smokers are also adversely affected. When parents smoke in the presence of their children, they put them in physical danger. When office workers light up, they put their colleagues in peril. When people puff tobacco in automobiles, they threaten those with them.

Those who gather facts and figures about world hunger make it clear that cigarettes are a major factor contributing to starvation and malnutrition among the millions of people in the Two-Thirds nations. They know that if the land that is presently being used to grow tobacco in these poor nations of Latin America were used to grow food, the hunger problem would be reduced significantly.

Smoking is addictive. It causes people to become slaves to their appetites. It harms the body. It endangers the lives of others. It contributes to world hunger. It diminishes spirituality. It is a curse that is encouraged for economic reasons. It is a practice tolerated by the church. So far as I am concerned, the craving for tobacco is another form of gluttony and the Christian community ought to get tough about it. Why is it that secular agencies like the American Medical Association and the American Cancer Society have more to say against smoking than the church does? Among Christian groups, only the Seventh Day Adventists have made an overt, concerted effort to denounce the use of tobacco and to provide extensive programs and counseling to help nicotine addicts to overcome their problem.

ALCOHOL

It is impossible for those who are in the grip of habitual drinking to follow the leading of God. There are countless stories of persons who have forfeited successful careers, marriages, familial happiness and even commitment to Christ as a result of their captivity to the bottle.

In one particular case, an attractive Christian couple who had been exceptionally successful in pastoring a church found themselves addicted to alcohol. Because they were serving a very conservative congregation, they were afraid to seek help. They could not risk having their problem made public. They made commitments to stop their drinking, but each of them secretly cheated on those commitments. Their problem became gradually worse, but still they resisted getting help. On several occasions, the absence of sobriety kept them out of pulpit. Eventually they gave up the pastorate and then completely severed their relationship to the church. Despair over their failure to conquer their drinking problem led them to doubt that they had any relationship with Christ. These tragic lives came to a more tragic end when, one night while under the influence of alcohol, they drove their car head-on into a tractor trailer and were killed.

Ironically, as our knowledge of the horrors of alcohol has increased, our toleration of alcohol has also increased. Baptist churches which once required their members to "abstain from the use of alcohol as a beverage" have generally deleted such prohibitions from their covenants. Many Methodist churches which once made abstinence part of their discipline now have nothing to say about drinking. By no means do I want to establish a new round of legalism in the evangelical community; yet, I do believe that the church must make it clear that substance abuse is a serious sin and that tobacco and alcohol are hindrances for those who long for spirituality.

Some of the more important discoveries which have come from the recent attention given to alcohol related problems center on the families of alcoholics. For instance, a woman married to an alcoholic who remains faithful to her husband and dedicated to raising her children properly can be regarded as a community heroine. People may stand in awe of her ability to hold her home together in spite of the fact that her husband drinks up the family income and abuses her. Church members may hold her up as an example of Christian womanhood who does her duty despite apparently insurmountable obstacles. It is easy to understand how such a woman might enjoy having the community and church view her in this way. Under such circumstances this woman might have a vested interest in maintaining the status quo.

Some wives have been found to do subtle things to keep their husbands "off the wagon." They may refuse to take a "get tough" posture which could force their husbands to seek work. They may make excuses for their husbands and protect them against the realities of their situations.

I know of one man who was wonderfully converted to Christ and, as a result of that conversion, took steps to overcome his drinking problem. His recovery from alcoholism was so dramatic that he gained a significant amount of public attention. Soon he was on the evangelical speaking circuit giving his testimony before adoring crowds. His wife, who previously had been treated as a saint by her fellow church members, went through a radical change of role definition which she found hard to accept. Now, instead of being regarded as a heroic woman who raised her children and sent them to college while married to an alcoholic, she came to be regarded as a lucky woman who was married to a wonderful husband. She found her new role devoid of the glorious status she formerly had enjoyed, and consequently unacceptable. After a couple of years, her husband fell from his lofty position as a popular speaker and went back to his old ways. When the full story was told, it was discovered that this woman had been largely responsible for his fall away from sobriety. At parties she had goaded him by ridiculing his teetotaling ways as pious and holier-than-thou. At home she had made alcohol constantly available, suggesting that one little drink from time to time would not hurt. Soon her husband was back to his being drunk much of the time.

Alcoholism not only affects the drinker, but also significantly disrupts the lives of family members. They also need help, and that is why a relatively new organization named Alanon has been created to supplement the good work of Alcoholics Anonymous. The church should not compete with either of these two splendid agencies for the job of rehabilitating alcoholics and their families. Recovered alcoholics do the best work with others who have drinking problems.

Only those who have had to deal with alcoholism in the daily experiences of their own lives are credible advisers for others who need such help. Both Alanon and Alcoholics Anonymous are religious in orientation, in that they require members to acknowledge that they are helpless when it comes to handling their own problems and must look to God for help. Both recognize that there must be a constant and on-going vigil against the temptations that have proved so destructive in the past, and that only a day-by-day reliance on God will give alcoholics the strength to be conquerors.

It is a good thing for churches to establish cooperative ties with both Alcoholics Anonymous and Alanon. Many churches have offered the use of their facilities to these organizations for meetings and have gained members from A.A. and Alanon as a result of their cooperative and sympathetic attitude. The church can learn many lessons from these organizations which have so effectively helped people with alcohol-related problems. The care that the members give one another is like the care that Christians should exercise for each other. These two groups demonstrate magnificently how members of a caring body should constantly be available to one another. But perhaps the most important thing the church can learn from Alcoholics Anonymous and Alanon is that personal problems related to addiction do not have private or individual solutions. Whether the problem is with food, or cigarettes, or alcohol, personal resolve is seldom, if ever, the answer. These groups have demonstrated that those with gluttonous appetites require a support group if they are to live victorious lives for Christ.

They help us to see that as crucial as it is for persons to turn over their lives to Christ and allow Him to do His saving work, most people need the contemporary body of Christ to undergird them. The maintenance of brothers and sisters under the lordship of Christ is highly dependent on there being a body of Christ's disciples who are willing to bear one another's burdens and so fulfill the law of Christ (Gal. 6:2).

CHAPTER SEVEN

GREED

OUR SOCIETY has built its economy on the production of things that people are conditioned to want, but do not really need. Many of the consumer goods we spend so much to buy did not even exist a generation ago. We buy these things because we have been manipulated into wanting them through advertising and peer pressure.

We are willing to work two jobs in order to satisfy these artificially created wants. We are willing to take time from our families so that we can buy those things which we are assured will express our love to our loved ones more than our mere presence ever could. We are willing to reject biblical principles of living in order to buy the consumer goods which the media prescribes as essential for the "good life." And when there are threats to the affluent lifestyle that has become synonymous with America, we stand ready to fight and, if need be, to die to protect it.

If our greedy consumption of oil is challenged by the OPEC nations, we do whatever is necessary in order to keep the oil flowing into our tanks. If totalitarian dictatorships or oppressive racist regimes promote policies which help us sustain our overly consumptive way of life, we support those dictatorships and tolerate those oppressive racist regimes. Our greedy materialistic way of life drives us to compromise principles of justice, yield on the canons of morality, and even to lose our souls.

Needs are fixed and limited, but artificially generated wants know no limits. Just when we get what we think we want, we see some new and "better" things. God has provided enough to satisfy all our needs, but not enough to satisfy all our artificially created wants. Of the getting of things, there will be no end.

Greed motivates people to buy things just for the sake of having them. It gives the possessors a deluded sense of superiority. Somehow we think that we are better than other people if we have more things than they do. In our materialistic society, children get sucked into this delusion from their earliest days. At Christmastime, they are taught that the better a person is, the more that person gets. Therefore, each child tries to point out how many more things he/she received from Santa than were delivered to the homes of playmates.

When I was a child, late on Christmas Day my sisters and I would run to the homes of our friends to play the game of "What did you get?" We would pretend that our presents were bigger and better than theirs, because we were convinced that the better children got the best things. And if we believed that we did not get better things than anyone else, we felt sad and envious, irregardless of how many gifts were under our tree.

We failed to realize that we could never have enough, because there would always be someone else out there with more. It did not occur to us that we would never be content until we had more than everyone else. Greed can never be satisfied. The more the greedy get, the more they want; and the more they want, the more discontented they are with what they have.

Some people do not outgrow the greediness they learn in childhood. Greed can linger on in disguised form, concealed by politeness, but eating away like a cancer at the joy of life. There is more truth than humor to the T-shirt message I saw, "Life is a game. Whosoever has the most things at the end wins." There are those in our churches who attempt to teach that the accumulation of things does not bring happiness, but such efforts are generally ineffective. It requires a miraculous conversion experience for most people to escape the belief that getting things is what life is all about.

When the affluent lifestyle of Americans is attacked these days, there is usually an immediate reaction interpreting the attack as a call for people to live lives of impoverishment. Yet there is little doubt in my mind that those who have felt a call to sell what they have and give to the poor have adopted a lifestyle that is very much in accord with the teachings of Scripture, if it is carried out for the right motives.

St. Francis of Assisi is still esteemed as one of the great figures in Christian history and is a worthy model for all of us, Protestant and Catholic alike. A valid Christian lifestyle of this modern age is exemplified in Mother Teresa. There is more to the simple lifestyle of this modern day saint than the good works that have come from her self-giving. She has learned what I have not yet succeeded in learning: "You will never know that Jesus is all you need, until Jesus is all you've got." Those who become poor as they respond to the needs of others are blessed in ways that those who live more greedy lives will never know. Those who *choose* poverty for the sake of others are blessed by Jesus and promised that they will be the inheritors of the kingdom of God (Luke 6:20).

The most haunting passage of Scripture for me is 1 John 3:17. There the Apostle John asks: "But whoso hath this world's good, and seeth his brother have need, and shutteth up his bowels of compassion from him, how dwelleth the love of God in him?" (KJV) I do not like to think about that simple question, but when I do, I find myself doubting my claims that I am on my way to becoming a sanctified Christian. I wonder how it is possible to hold on to the things that I want, but do not need, when other persons created by God are in desperate need. I ask myself how much I really love Jesus when I, like the rich young ruler, hold on to "great possessions," while so many languish in their poverty.

I have no easy responses to questions like these. I try to assure myself that I am saved by *grace*, not by good works (Eph. 2:8), but then I wonder if I have cheapened grace, as Dietrich Bonhoeffer once suggested, by refusing it the opportunity to lead me into a Christlike lifestyle in regard to the poor.

KINGDOM PERSPECTIVES

Among the ancient Jews there was a hope for shalom. This word was used not only as part of the greeting and parting expressions which marked the encounters of Jewish friends; it also carried the image of the kind of world in which they longed for all people to live. The word *shalom,* commonly translated "peace," meant something far more than "peace of mind" to the people of Israel. It conveyed the image of living in a caring community in which there would be no greed and all people would care for one another even as God cares. To the Jews, *shalom* was what we Christians call the kingdom of God—a society in which everyone has enough of everything needed for joyful living.

There were symbols of shalom in the life of Israel that condemned the greediness lurking in the hearts of the ungodly. One of its clearest expressions is found in the story of the Exodus. When the Jews escaped from Egypt and wandered in the wilderness, God saw to it that they had enough to eat. Manna was sent from heaven so that each of the Children of Israel might have enough food for the day. Moses warned against greediness and told the Jews that if they took more than they needed, the surplus would decay and be filled with worms. Those who did not follow the directives of God found that things were just as Moses had predicted (Ex. 16). In shalom there is enough for everyone, but surplus for no one. That which is surplus rots.

The New Testament gives us a similar kind of warning. In the Gospel of Luke, we read:

And He spake a parable unto them, saying,

"The ground of a certain rich man brought forth plentifully: And he thought within himself saying, 'What shall I do, because I have no room where to bestow my fruits?' And he said, 'This will I do: I will pull down my barns, and build greater; and there will I bestow all my fruits and my goods. And I will say to my soul, "Soul, thou has goods laid up for many years; take thine ease, eat, drink and be merry." '

"But God said unto him, 'Thou fool, this night thy soul shall be required of thee; then whose shall those things be, which thou hast provided?' "

"So is he that layeth up treasure for himself, and is not rich toward God" (Luke 12:16-21, KJV).

Jesus establishes clearly that the greedy accumulation of things is an attempt by persons to evade dependency on God. The one who greedily hoards possessions in order to establish security for the future lacks the faith that Jesus expects of those who follow Him. Our security, according to Jesus, is in our relationship to God in whose hands lies our future. Because of the uncertainty of life, it is ridiculous to be greedy hoarders of things. The will of God is that each of us should have enough and then be willing to offer up our surplus to others in the name of God. There is no room for greed in the shalom of the ancient Jews or in the kingdom envisioned by modern Christians.

In the ideal society set forth in the Bible, all persons are to "fit in" with others and with the natural environment. There is harmony in all things. No one enjoys abundance at the expense of others. No one lives in a way that threatens the ecological balance. In everything that any person does, there is consideration for all others. In the Peaceable Kingdom which is to come at the second coming of Christ, each will live in an appropriate manner, consuming enough, but never more than is just in relationship to others.

THE EUCHARISTIC LIFESTYLE

John Taylor, the Bishop of Winchester, England, in his book, *Enough Is Enough,* calls Christians to "eucharistic living." He shows the dimensions of the lifestyle prescribed by the Mosaic Law, which gives insights on how we should live. Taylor points out that once a year, at Passover, all Jewish families brought one-tenth of all that they possessed (not simply one-tenth of their annual income) to Jerusalem to be offered up to God.

These gifts were not to be used for maintaining outreach programs or to sustain the local religious establishment. This vast accumulation of wealth was not designated for what we might call "some worthy cause." Instead, this incredible collection was used for a party. That's right! A party! All the people of Israel were expected to travel to Jerusalem and participate in a gigantic blowout party at which one-tenth of all the assets of the nation's population would be spent on a banquet of celebration. There was singing and dancing. Every person from every corner of Israel was invited, and none would be turned away. The village idiot, the tax collector, those of questionable reputation, the poor, the rich, the educated, and the uncouth bums—they were all to be there. The music would play into the nights as the party went on for days.

No wonder the Children of Israel said, "I was glad when they said unto me, 'Let us go unto the house of the Lord.' " In ancient Israel, God was worshiped in celebration. That is important for us to remember in our contemporary situation. The kingdom of God is more like party than a soup kitchen. It is good for us to read the instructions of Moses on the way that our God requires that we enjoy Him:

> Thou shalt truly tithe all the increase of thy seed, that the field bringeth forth year by year.
>
> And thou shalt eat before the Lord thy God, in the place which He shall choose to place His name there,

the tithe of thy corn, of thy wine, and of thine oil, and the firstlings of the herds and of thy flocks; that thou mayest learn to fear the Lord thy God always. And if the way be too long for thee, so that thou art not able to carry it; if the place be too far from thee, which the Lord thy God shall choose to set His name there, when the Lord thy God hath blessed thee; Then shalt thou turn it into money, and bind up the money in thine hand, and shalt go unto the place which the Lord thy God shall choose: And thou shalt bestow that money for whatsoever thy soul lusteth after, for oxen, or for sheep, or for wine, or for strong drink, or for whatsoever thy soul desireth: and thou shalt eat there before the Lord thy God, and thou shalt rejoice, thou, and thine household.

And the Levite that is within thy gates; thou shalt not forsake him; for he hath no part nor inheritance with thee (Deut. 14:22-27, KJV)

Knowing that our God loves celebrations, I am delivered from a dour lifestyle in which I am made to feel guilty whenever I have a good time. I can enjoy a trip to the beach with friends, scream with excitement at a basketball game, and eat a good meal without going through a period of self-condemnation for having spent what could have been used to feed the poor. Our God loves a party, and those who refuse to party in His name lose out on a foretaste of glory that is to be when His kingdom comes on earth as it is in heaven.

The important lesson to be learned from all of this is that there are limitations on partying. Moses teaches us that one-tenth of our assets in any given year must be set aside for partying, and the other nine-tenths are to be used in service for others in the name of the Lord. There's nothing wrong with spending a dollar or two on a roller coaster ride (our God enjoys sharing a good time with us) as long as we keep our spending on pleasure under control.

As we respond to the needs of the poor, we must remember this admonition of Jesus:

> Moreover when ye fast, be not as the hypocrites, of a sad countenance; for they disfigure their faces, that they may appear unto men to fast. Verily I say unto you, They have their reward. But thou, when thou fastest, anoint thine head, and wash thy face; That thou appear not unto men to fast, but unto thy Father which is in secret: and thy Father, which seeth in secret, shall reward thee openly (Matthew 6:16-18, KJV).

Sacrifices are to be made for the poor, but our lifestyles should give evidence that we are happy, party-going disciples of the One who invites us to a banquet. There is nothing wrong with dressing up as long as we limit what we spend.

Unfortunately, most of us have turned the Lord's formula around. We spend nine-tenths of what we possess on the party and things we want for ourselves and, if we are tithers, the remaining tenth on service for His kingdom. God wants His people to enjoy life, but He wants us to enjoy life in a manner that does not require the suffering of others. He does not want any of us to adopt a lifestyle that leads to the disproportionate consumption of the good things that God meant for all of His children to enjoy.

GREED AND INTERNATIONAL PROBLEMS

In today's world, greed is not a sin which merely influences our personal relationships; it also is responsible for many of the pressing international problems which seem to defy solution. Those of us confined to spaceship earth are being thrust into an uncertain future, threatened by such ugly specters as a nuclear holocaust, a third World War, the starvation of half a billion people, and political totalitarianism. As we think about such possibilities, we must stop and consider the observations of James, who tells us that wars and conflicts of all sorts come from the greed of people trying to get what they do not need, but desperately want (see James 4:1-3). The resources of the earth are limited and, if certain people demand more than their just share of things, the consequences will be horrendous.

Lately a number of Christian authors have written on the question, "Is capitalism Christian?" The attempts to answer this question have been scholarly and well developed, but some of these writers fail to perceive that the question is wrong. What we should be asking is, "How can we make capitalism Christian? Every principality and power in our world, as well as every individual, is in a fallen state and is in need of restoration to the state that God intended. Capitalism can be made to glorify God if those who are part of such an economic system are willing to free it from elements of greed. Contemporary proponents of capitalism readily admit that greed is a part of this economic system in its present form. In the book *Essays in Persuasion,* Maynard Keynes, one of the foremost theorists of modern day capitalism, states:

> For at least another hundred years we must pretend to ourselves and to everyone that fair is foul and foul is fair; for foul is useful and fair is not. Avarice and usury and precaution must be our gods for a little longer still. For only they can lead us out of the tunnel of economic necessity into daylight (W.W. Norton Co., Inc. 1963, p. 372).

Such statements are hard to reconcile with the ethics of the Bible. It is the task of those of us who see the possibilities for human freedom and social progress inherent in capitalism to redeem it from the potential for greed which is also inherent within it. At a time in human history when capitalism offers more hope for good than the available alternatives, it becomes a matter of urgency that this economic system be brought under the judgment of God so that it can be purged and made to be as good as it can be.

We must not think that the abuses of capitalism are confined to the robber barons of bygone days. The greed that motivated those tyrants of business and industry who lived at the turn of the century lies in the hearts of all of us. There are those today who would destructively exploit the environment and bring suffering to others in order to gratify their craving for financial gain.

A case in point can be found in a recent plan for a project to be developed in the heart of Brazil. The Amazon jungle, according to some experts, is producing through photosynthesis approximately 20 percent of all the world's oxygen. A billionaire has purchased 500,000 acres of the Amazon in order to turn its trees into wood pulp. With a pulp plant manufactured in Japan and towed 15,000 miles to a tributary of the Amazon River, he expects to produce 750 metric tons of pulp every day. This would be enough pulp to produce sufficient toilet paper daily to go around the world sixteen times. We have to question whether the private enterprise of one individual can justify endangering the well-being of everyone on the planet. The significance of this project becomes particularly noteworthy when a study of the recent drought in Africa reveals that it may be the result of ecological imbalances which have occurred recently in the Amazon River systems. Evidently the destruction of the jungle has disturbed the processes which create rain, and the prevailing winds no longer have rain clouds to carry to the African continent.

In a case closer to home, we have witnessed the greed of some to exploit our dependency on fossil fuels. According to a study conducted by a Pulitzer Prize winning writer for the Philadelphia *Inquirer,* a few oil companies deliberately functioned as an oligopoly and manipulated the price of oil upward more than 150 percent. There are those who argue that the oil companies should get whatever the market will allow, in spite of the fact that such price manipulations have left poor people without heating fuel and many of the inner-city elderly in real danger of freezing to death. I say that Christians must save the capitalistic system from such evil practices or else capitalism will be destroyed. Even as the Prophet Jeremiah condemned his king for building a palace at the expense of the poor (Jer. 22:13-17), so we must be ready to stand against those greedy people whose business practices exploit the poor in our time. We need scholars who will show us how to keep capitalism from destroying us. Saint Thomas Aquinas once taught, "A contract is fair when both parties gain equally." The time has come for the church to spell out for those in business the nature of fair contractual relationships according to biblical principles.

GREED IN UNIONS

Greed expresses itself not only among the entrepreneurs who create the businesses and industries which generate jobs, but also among the workers who are employed in these jobs. There was a time when workers were controlled and manipulated unfairly by their bosses. They worked incredibly long hours, under subhuman conditions for unbelievably low wages. Their children and wives were forced to work to supplement the family income which, in most cases, was close to the subsistence level. Conditions for the labor force became so unbearable that workers were willing to take risks and make sacrifices to change the social arrangements which had reduced them to exploited victims. Out of these desperate conditions the labor movement was born. Inspired by a vision of a more just economic order, the workers in industries and businesses across the nation organized into unions that were able to achieve great benefits for their workers through collective bargaining. Largely as a result of the union movement, the American workers have become the highest paid in the world.

Today the future of those in the labor force is threatened not by exploitive employers but by their own greed. Certainly, there are a variety of reasons for the collapse of many American industries, not the least of which is poor management. However, one of the significant causes of the loss of jobs due to the closing down of factories here in the United States is the avarice of American union members. At times, they seem almost to will their own destruction as they strike for wages that are so unreasonable that employers are forced to take their operations out of the country to a place where labor is cheaper. It is time for us to recognize that our capitalistic system is in danger, not only because of the greed of the industrialists, but because of the greed of workers who demand more and more pay for less and less work.

Christians need a new philosophy of money. In *The London Times,* one of the leading churchmen of England wrote:

> The demand for "fairness" in prices and incomes suggests some convictions that there are, or should be, some moral considerations in the distribution of the rewards of industry and the market price should not be the sole criterion. We should ask, what is "fair?" What does a man deserve?

The greediness of workers is evident in the fact that unions no longer advocate shorter work days because they know that if their members had more time off, they would probably take second jobs and thereby reduce the number of jobs available for the unemployed. Furthermore, these union members who have gained so much for themselves through collective bargaining show all too little sympathy and provide all too little support for the Latino farm workers who have become an oppressed underclass in our affluent society. The Old Testament prophets would have as much to say to the union members of America as they would have to say to the tycoons who exploit the poor.

GREED AND PROPHECY

The Book of Revelation tells us that the kingdom of evil stands in opposition to the kingdom of God. John labeled this diabolical social order "Babylon." In Revelation 13-18, we read of the sins of Babylon that bring about its ultimate destruction. Babylon, says the Scripture, is the great whore that seduces people (Rev. 17:1-5). It is a beastly creature which demands worship (13:4). And it is a city which greedily consumes the resources of the world (18:7-13).

When I was a teenager, I loved to go to church and hear prophecy sermons that decoded the secret symbols of the vision of John. The Gospels were okay, but I felt that the deep stuff in the Book of Revelation lay waiting to be discovered by "brilliant" minds. The Bible teachers who led these prophecy conferences always seemed able to explain world events from this most mysterious book of the Bible. Babylon, they said, was the Soviet Union. They seemed able to correlate the behavior of the leading nation of the Marxist movement with the descriptions of the Great Whore outlined in Revelation 4–18. It was interesting to learn from my father that, during the 1930s, similar preachers considered Germany to be Babylon. Furthermore, I have since learned that certain evangelical preachers in Latin America consider the United States to be that evil nation.

In the last few years, I have come to believe that Babylon may refer to any society. For me, Babylon represents any socio-economic system that is not under the lordship of Christ. If Christians are living in Russia, then Russia is their Babylon. For Christians living in Britain, Britain is their Babylon. For Mexicans, Mexico is Babylon and for those of us who are Americans, the United States is Babylon. The kingdom of God is represented by the New Jerusalem (Rev. 21:2) which God sends from heaven to take the place of the old dying order.

Once I began to apply the Scripture to my own situation, it seemed to be alive with meaning. I saw my own affluent society as the seductive whore drawing Christians away from God by offering them an array of worldly delights (Rev.17–18). Who of us can deny that we sense the seduction of our culture which in a host of subtle, and not so subtle, ways lures us into striving greedily after its pleasures.

Our society, furthermore, like the Babylon of prophecy, requires that we worship her. Nationalism, here as elsewhere in the world, is easily transformed into a religion, and patriotism is at times unconsciously enthroned into worship of the state. Satan enjoys perverting that which is good and using it for his purposes, so it is no surprise that emotions like patriotism, which can bring out the best in us, can be twisted in such a way that we become jingoistic, ethnocentric national chauvinists.

Lastly and most importantly, I recognize that our society, like the Babylon of the Bible, encourages wasteful overconsumption which will eventually seal its doom.

> And the kings of earth, who have committed fornication and lived deliciously with her, shall bewail her, and lament for her, when they shall see the smoke of her burning. Standing afar off for the fear of her torment, saying, "Alas, alas that great city Babylon, that mighty city! For in one hour is thy judgment come."
>
> And the merchants of the earth shall weep and mourn over her; for no man buyeth their merchandise any more; the merchandise of gold, and silver, and precious stones, and of pearls, and fine linen, and purple, and silk and scarlet, and all thyine wood, and all manner vessels of ivory, and all manner vessels of most precious wood, and of brass, and iron, and marble, and cinnamon, and odors, and ointments and frankincense, and wine, and oil, and fine flour, and wheat, and beasts, and sheep, and horses, and chariots, and slaves, and souls of men. And the fruits that

thy soul lusted after are departed from thee, and all
things which were dainty and goodly are departed
from thee, and thou shalt find them no more at all
(Rev.18:9-14, KJV).

I believe that unless we Americans are able to find in Christ
deliverance from our greedy and wasteful lifestyle, our nation
is doomed to suffer the fate of Babylon. Our greed, which has
resulted in untold suffering among the poor peoples of the
world, is known to God, and He will respond to our evil ways
on the day when He judges the nations (Matt. 25:32).

Consider the fact that one of the reasons there is hunger in
the world is that we have been seduced by our society to
develop tastes and appetites that require the exploitation of
farmland. If all the land in Latin America presently used to
grow sugar, coffee, and tobacco (all of which poison our
bodies and destroy our health) were used to grow food for
indigenous populations, empty stomachs would be filled and
dying children would be saved. Most of the food grown in
Third World countries is exported to richer countries. It is
heartbreaking to learn that most of the cattle butchered in
Latin America end up as hamburgers in the fast-food restau-
rants in the United States, while many of the people who
watched those cattle get fattened for the slaughter suffer from
malnutrition. The anchovy fisheries of Peru, with one-sixth of
the world's fish production, export most of their catch to feed
the pets of North Americans. In the United States, we spend
$5 billion a year to feed 48 million dogs and 28 million cats.
Please understand that I love animals and have a well-fed cat
in my home, but I wonder what our Lord's judgment will be
on a society in which 80 percent of its dogs are deemed
overweight while the poor of the world starve to death.

The excesses of our society make for frightening statistics.
We buy what we do not need and throw away what we no
longer want. We junk 7 million cars each year, 70,000 of
which are abandoned on the streets of New York City. We

throw away 52 billion aluminum cans and 24 billion bottles. One of the most serious problems of modern American is the disposal of the waste materials that result from our greedy lifestyles. All of this greed and waste becomes intolerable in the face of the following facts:

- One billion people go to sleep hungry each night.
- 40,000 people die of starvation each day.
- Out of every 100 babies born in the world, 40 will risk permanent physical and/or mental damage because of malnutrition, and only 3 out of the 100 will get the education and skills they need to perform creative work.
- More than 100,000 children go blind every year due to lack of vitamin A in their diets.

The greed of the American population is one major factor contributing to these tragedies. The time has come to repent and to abandon the ways of Babylon. The time has come to heed the Book of Revelation, which says:

> "Come out of her, my people, that ye be not partakers of her sins, and that ye receive not of her plagues. For her sins have reached unto heaven and God hath remembered her iniquities" (18:4-5, KJV).

OVERCOMING GREED

There is one primary way to overcome greed, and that is to discover the joy that comes from self-giving. The nature of sin is that it blinds us to the truth that we have been designed in the image of a giving God (John 3:16), and that we therefore fulfill the purpose of our Creator by giving away what we are and have to others. When we are called upon to sacrifice, it is not only that others might benefit from our self-giving, but that we ourselves might know the joy that God wills for us to have. If we do not experience a sense of wondrous fulfillment in our giving, then the Lord would rather that we reconsider what we do and why we do it (2 Cor. 9:7).

God is quite able to meet the needs of the poor without us if He so chooses, but instead He has created a world that allows all of us to realize the greatest happiness that life can afford. This happiness comes from giving what He has placed in our hands to meet the needs of those who are in desperate straits.

I know of a family that made a commitment to support several poor children in Haiti. A little more than $100 dollars a month was sufficient to feed, clothe, and educate five orphan children who otherwise would have had no hope. In order for the family to carry out its commitment, there were sacrifices to be made. The children had to forego some of the things that many of their friends took for granted. They rode secondhand bicycles and sometimes their Christmas presents did not compare favorably with what their friends got. The family, nevertheless, stayed with their commitment for almost a decade.

One day the father of this family came home with some exciting news. His company was sending him to Haiti for a week to take care of some business matters. Because his way would be paid by his company, he would be able to take his family along, provided they traveled in the most economical way possible. The family was thrilled with the possibility of meeting the five children whom they had supported for such a long time.

The second day they were in Haiti, the family hired a jeep and drove out to the village where their young friends lived. The children, who were now teenagers, had been told of the visit and looked forward eagerly to the day when they would meet those who had done so much for them. The American family traveled for hours, but their tiredness did not detract from the joy they experienced when they arrived at their destination.

The five young people whom they had supported stood waiting in front of their school. They had been there since the early morning waiting to meet their American friends. As soon as the jeep stopped in front of the school, the five Haitian teenagers ran to it with happy excitement. The two American children bounced out of the jeep and into their arms and there followed a quarter-hour of glorious hugging. Despite the language barrier, these young people communicated their affection for each other. At the end of that special day there was an unplanned ceremony in which the Haitian children gave to their American friends Christmas tree ornaments they themselves had made out of twigs and sisal. After a long and affectionate good-bye, the Americans got back into their jeep to return to Port-au-Prince.

On the way to the capital city, the two children sat in pensive silence. Their silence seemed so strange and puzzling that their father asked what was wrong. "Oh, nothing's wrong," answered his daughter. "I was just thinking that there is nothing we could have done with our money over the last ten years that would have made us happier than we are right now."

There are many good Christian organizations that can help to establish relationships with children in poor countries who are in need of support. One of the best is Compassion International, a highly evangelical relief organization. For $21 a month, Compassion International can arrange for the support of a child whose life otherwise would be lived out in desperation. Twenty-one dollars a month is approximately seventy cents a day—the cost of a cup of coffee. The address of Compassion International is 3955 Cragwood Drive, P.O. Box 7000, Colorado Springs, Colorado 80933.

In 1979, a rich man was asked to deliver a commencement address to his old elementary school in Harlem, New York City. In the course of his remarks, he spontaneously made a fantastic offer to the boys and girls of the graduating class. He offered to pay the tuition of any of the children who wanted to go to college. The children responded to the offer with enthusiasm and this rich man delivered on his promise, and then some. He not only provided the necessary funds, but he also made a commitment of his time to these children. As the years went by, he counseled and tutored them. His visits and encouragement were crucial in getting these children through high school. His loving support and financial assistance have carried most of them into college.

The story of this generous millionaire would be incomplete without stating the fact that this man had more genuine joy from what he gave to these young people than he ever could have derived from either greedily hoarding his wealth or spending it on his own pleasures. Greediness promises much, but delivers little in the way of joy. On the other hand, those who are lovingly self-giving discover the real joy that money and things can give if they are graciously shared with others. This may seem a bit simplistic, but it is, nevertheless, the truth. Greed is defeated in the face of the hilarious joy that comes from Christlike giving.

A WARNING TO YUPPIES

Yuppies is the name ascribed to the generation of young people who are taking their places in the business world of the 1980s, the *Y*oung, *U*rban *P*rofessionals. A study made by *Fortune* magazine revealed some disturbing things about this group of Americans. The young people are intensely committed to living what they consider to be the "good life." When questioned about what they considered that to be, they responded that the "good life" is a lifestyle in which a person can enjoy good things. Their goals included making enough money to buy gourmet foods, own expensive cars (preferably BMWs), live in pleasant surroundings, and vacation in exotic places. In order to reach these goals, they are willing to make necessary trade-offs in their personal lives. They will forego marriage until they can be sure it will not interfere with their money-making careers. None of those interviewed intend to have children because they see children as an inconvenience and an interference with their career goals. These Yuppies feel no loyalties or obligations except to themselves. They view their employers as means to an end, their jobs as stepping-stones to better positions, and the families into which they were born as persons who "act like something is owed to them." In young adults, greediness has become a way of life. Unfortunately, our churches are preparing teenagers to take their places in this self-serving system, teaching that this is what decent American Christian young people ought to do.

I guess it is a good thing that Yuppies aren't too high on marriage. There is little doubt in my mind that greedy persons make poor marital partners. They seem to be interested only in what they get out of the marriage and have little concern for what they can contribute in love. There is more and more talk of "symbiotic" relationships in which the self-centered interests of one member offer an unintentional benefit which serves the self-centered interests of the other. More and more couples anticipating marriage draw up marriage contracts so that each may protect and keep what they own, and gain the maximum advantage from the marital arrangement.

Contrast the Yuppies with a young woman who is far from typical of our young adult population. After completing college, she sought out organizations which might offer her an opportunity to give her life in meaningful service to others. Following several interviews and study tours, she decided to work with an organization called Habitat for Humanity.

She was particularly drawn to this organization because of its founder, Millard Fuller. She learned that he himself had once been seduced by Babylon into a lifestyle of affluence. He had learned how to make money better than most people ever do and before he had turned thirty, he had become a millionaire. His success nurtured his greed and he seldom stopped to enjoy what he had earned. He hurled himself with increasing zeal into new ventures which promised more money and greater opportunities for investments. Then one day, unexpectedly, his wife told him that she was leaving him. The news shook him to the depths of his being and forced him to reevaluate his life and the things for which he had lived. Consequently, he took a step that would launch him into a form of missionary service which would change his life, give a new beginning to his marriage, and bring hope to thousands of poor people. He decided to help the poor build decent housing for themselves. Fuller sold all his possessions and, along with his wife, became committed to working on the mission. First in Africa, later in Latin America and eventually in the United States, he organized poor people to work along with members of his organization in order to build housing that would allow them to live with dignity.

Habitat for Humanity makes the funds needed for building materials available through no interest loans. Fuller believes that the Bible teaches that loans to the poor should not entail interest. Habitat workers receive no salary, and get little public recognition for their long hours of service. But they radiate a joy that can only be regarded as the joy of Christ.

Today the young woman of our story is working joyfully with people who are blessed by the vision of a decent life. She is enthusiastic and excited about her vocation. She has learned the rewards of a sacrificial lifestyle that is marked by more than what have become the tribal practices of evangelicals. We must teach that it is not enough to give up obscene rock music, "R" rated movies, and beer parties. We must communicate to a lost generation that being a Christian is rejecting Babylon and becoming a citizen of the New Jerusalem. It is turning one's back on greediness and allowing Jesus to create a heart of self-giving in its place.

AFTERWORD

THE REWARD FOR SHEDDING the old nature and leaving behind the motivations generated by the Seven Deadly Sins is not in what we get, but in what we become. Holiness is its own reward. As holiness is realized, there is a taste of joy to life that cannot be known in any other way. The fragmentation of consciousness which characterizes so many of us in this helter-skelter world is reversed, and we come to know an inner peace which passes all understanding. As we are being freed from the old nature, so carefully delineated by those who first outlined the Seven Deadly Sins, we are being freed to love in new and vital ways. As we set aside these "weights that do so easily beset us," we are liberated to give ourselves emotionally to one another. The fulfillment that comes from loving becomes part of our experience. We become more fully human as we enter into the blessings of being in Christ and become persons who no longer make allowance for the flesh.

During the last decade, the evangelical community in America has become justifiably concerned about the encroachment of secular humanism in the American ideology. To claim that there are no values other than those which human beings establish through societal interaction can only lead to an ethical relativism which leaves people devoid of solid principles for living. However, we must be careful lest, in the attacks on secular humanism, we lose sight of the fact that it is God's will for all of us to realize the potentiality of our humanity. To be human is to be made in the image of God, and the more we conform to His image the more we become human. Humanness is realized when we are delivered from our sinfulness through a personal relationship with Jesus. Our Lord was not only the perfect incarnation of God, but was also the incarnation of perfect humanity. The humanness which He expressed when He walked among us 2,000 years ago is the ultimate humanness for which all people hunger. In Him are the qualities of a new humanity. "But the fruit of the Spirit is love, joy, peace, patience, kindness, goodness, faithfulness, gentleness, self-control; against such there is no law" (Gal. 5:22-23).

Jesus came into the world, not only to deliver us from the punishment for sin, but to make of us a new people. "If because of one man's trespass, death reigned through that one man, much more will those who receive the abundance of grace and the free gift of righteousness reign in life through the one man Jesus Christ" (Rom. 5:17).

By surrendering to Christ's resurrected presence which is known to us as the Holy Spirit, and by making a commitment to allow Him to help us overcome the presence of the Seven Deadly Sins in our lives, we will come to realize the new humanity which God intended for us from the beginning of creation. We must not allow representatives of anti-Christian human potential movements to usurp essential vocabulary and phraseology which enable us to express significant dimensions of biblical salvation. There is a new humanity in Christ, and only those who, by His grace, overcome the Seven Deadly Sins in their lives will become all that they can be.